"I can't say enough good things about the n
is a holistic guide to a career in real estate. After a long hiatus, I was
fortunate to renew my real estate career with Brad as my broker. His
advice and direction, as included in this book, have been invaluable.
Wisdom is included not only about the professional aspects of real
estate but the personal and relational impact of the work. My real
estate career has been successfully relaunched and invigorated thanks
to his advice. This book distills the wisdom of a seasoned realtor,
broker, investor, and mentor. Nothing beats working with Brad
personally, but this book is the next best thing."

—Debbie Hyde,
Agent

"This is a practical and inspirational guide to help realtors achieve
success in their business. The principles can also be applied across
many walks of life, making it a practical guide for anyone wanting
to achieve their highest potential. I especially like the 'Bonus Tips'
included at the end of each chapter. I highly recommend this as a
motivational tool for the new agent as well as the seasoned agent."

—Tracy Kamprath,
Broker

"It is my pleasure to recommend *The Mental Game of Real Estate* by
Brad Bevers. This is an excellent read for anyone in the real estate
industry. I've worked with Brad over the years, and his one-of-a-kind
character has always been something to admire. Brad continually
goes the extra mile and strives to help others grow. Read this book
and learn from the best!"

—DeeAnna Marek,
Realtor

"I sure wish this book had been available to me when I started my real estate career! I had to learn so many of these things by trial and error or just the plain old 'hard way.' Great advice and actionable steps for new agents, and even some good systems and processes in here for more seasoned agents!"

—Shelly Moschak,
Broker Associate, Farm & Ranch Real Estate Instructor

THE MENTAL GAME OF
REAL ESTATE

HOW TO THRIVE AS A REAL ESTATE AGENT

BRAD BEVERS

LUCIDBOOKS

The Mental Game of Real Estate
How to Thrive as a Real Estate Agent

Copyright © 2019 by Brad Bevers

Published by Lucid Books in Houston, TX
www.LucidBooksPublishing.com

ISBN-10: 1-63296-371-X
ISBN-13: 978-1-63296-371-0
eISBN-10: 1-63296-361-2
eISBN-13: 978-1-63296-361-1

Scripture quotations are taken from the ESV® Bible (The Holy Bible, English Standard Version®), copyright © 2001 by Crossway, a publishing ministry of Good News Publishers. Used by permission. All rights reserved.

Special Sales: Most Lucid Books titles are available in special quantity discounts. Custom imprinting or excerpting can also be done to fit special needs. Contact Lucid Books at Info@LucidBooksPublishing.com.

Table of Contents

Introduction   1

Head Start: Six Keys to Starting Strong   3

Mindset of a Real Estate Agent

Energy vs. Time   11

Taking the Long View   27

Everyone Is Selling Something   29

The 80/20 Agent   35

First Impressions   41

It's All Your Fault   45

Goals, Habits, and Following Through

Scheduling for Success   51

Taking Action   63

Real Estate Psychology 101

Real Estate and Influence   73

The Psychology of Negotiation   99

How to Always Get a Full Commission   115

Three Closing Techniques   125

Searching for the Best Clients   137

Common Contract Issues   143

The #1 Secret to Real Estate Success   153

The Four Ways to Make Money on a Property   159

Now . . . Go Sell Some Property   173

Recommended Reading   175

Notes   181

About the Author   183

Introduction

By the end of this book, you will have the tools to implement a long-term strategy for your real estate career, but you will also learn specific tactics you can use right away. My goal is to give you at least a hundred times the value you paid for this book.

Take what you learn from these pages and then experiment with other tactics until you develop your own. This method of development and testing will point you in the right direction and help you earn a living much faster than you would otherwise.

As you develop what works for you, it will be easy to focus on outcomes rather than doing the right things each day. An outcome bias is the mistaken assumption that the outcome determines whether an action was right or wrong. For example, we often assume that if something ends up succeeding, we made the right decision by acting on it. This belief is one of the largest flaws in our thinking as humans.

We should instead strive to have a gambler's mentality, recognizing that making the right decision mathematically may not lead to a positive outcome. Just because there's a 55 percent chance I will win if I split aces in blackjack, I'm not guaranteed to win. In real estate, as in life, even when you do all the right things, you won't always win. Keep your focus on implementing the right systems and continually setting yourself up for success.

Quit before You Start

When I meet with others asking for advice on whether they should become a real estate agent, I always tell them the same thing: "Don't do it unless you have to." If you have any other options, pursue those first. Real estate is a hard business—it takes a long time to build up a client base and establish a reputation.

I've seen a lot of agents start strong for a couple of years only to fizzle out because they didn't realize the kind of sacrifice required to build a real estate business. At a bare minimum, make sure you can confidently say at least one of the following:

1. I have five listings already lined up with friends and family, ready to go as soon as I hang my license with a broker.
2. I have saved up six months of income for what my family will need so that I can focus on growing my business the right way.
3. I have a steady paycheck and a job with enough flexibility that I can grow into my real estate career and transition when the time is right. I understand this will take longer, but it's my best option.
4. I have an understanding spouse who believes in real estate and is willing to support me as I get started.

My wife supported us for the first few years while I was beginning a career in real estate. I brought some money home, but it was too inconsistent to count on. Without my wife's support and belief, I never would have made it long enough in real estate to succeed.

If real estate is your dream, pursue it with all you have. But unless you have some money saved up or have other streams of income coming in, wait until the timing is right. Real estate is hard enough when you have those advantages; don't try to start without at least one of them in place.

Head Start:
Six Keys to Starting Strong

"Successful people do what unsuccessful people are not willing to do.
Don't wish it were easier, wish you were better."

—Jim Rohn

If I didn't talk you out of starting real estate in the introduction, here is what to know before going in to make sure you hit the ground running:

1. Have a financial cushion. Again, you should have a nest egg saved up or another job from which you can still earn money consistently as you get started. Commission sales take a long time to build up, and real estate can be unforgiving. Ideally, have a minimum of six months' expenses saved before starting down the real estate road.

   I didn't have anything saved when I started real estate at twenty-two years old, but I had a wife with a college degree who bought into the vision of what it would take to succeed. After seven years of barely getting by, we turned a corner and she was able to quit her job to stay home with our children when the business took off.

2. Avoid the quick-sale bug. There are many ways to make money in real estate—and just as many ways to ruin your career. Often, there are ways to make money and ruin your career at the same time. Don't take the easy path. Work on building up a client base who is loyal to you because you take better care of them than anyone else can. Stay in constant communication with them.

   Don't take short-term gains when they present themselves. There will always be a way to look out for yourself to the detriment of others; but if you have that mindset, you will never be successful in the long run. Building up a reputation for service and excellence is the best way to grow your business.

3. Don't just be an agent. As a real estate agent, you should be connected to many different groups and areas in the community. Your number one job, and the hardest thing to do as an agent, is to get in front of as many prospects as possible. Remember that sellers will interview fewer than three agents most of the time, and buyers usually work with whoever calls them back first.

   If you just focus on being an agent and spending time with other agents, you won't be building up the relationships that matter. Being a real estate agent is one of the best jobs in the world because no matter what you're interested in or where you're serving, you can build your business at the same time.

   Getting involved in various nonprofit groups in the community helped my business tremendously. Find a place where you truly enjoy serving, and that service may benefit your real estate business as well. I stumbled into this strategy by accident, but it's worth thinking through. Join an organization or group in which you are the only real estate agent, and then work to help grow it. This will pay off in the long run, and you won't have to contend with other agents who are already entrenched there.

4. Be an investor. What if I told you that you could increase your commissions tenfold? That instead of making 3 percent on a sale,

you could make 30 percent? Most agents are happy with just being an agent and helping their clients for the rest of their careers, but if you really want to grow your income and your reach, investing in property should be a priority.

You will learn the right way to invest and how to actually make money buying and selling real estate. This is invaluable information that you can pass on to your clients. There will be clients who don't want to work with you because you invest, but many more who see the value and want to be on your team. Here are some tips about investing:

- Investing will help you stand out among other agents. Look at the agents who invest in your local area. I guarantee that they are the top agents in their field.

- Investing gives you a chance to better your community and to do so publicly. I love taking a rundown house and fixing it up.

- Having your own properties means you have a definite listing when you decide to sell. Generating your own listings is a huge benefit.

- One word of warning: you must be extra vigilant not to neglect your duties as an agent in any way when you're an investor. I've passed on great deals before because jumping on them wouldn't have been fair to one client or another. My rule is that if I show a home to someone else, it's off the table for me until the client passes on it completely and I've asked them if they're okay if I pursue it myself.

- Investing puts you on the fast track to building up valuable relationships with banks in your area. Always try to use different banks so that you are building a reputation in multiple places. Stay local when you can. You may pay a slightly higher interest rate but building up local relationships will prove to be invaluable over time.

- What I look for in a flip: 70 percent ARV (after repair value). Here is what that looks like: let's say there is a house for sale that you think might be a good deal.
  - First, use your real estate knowledge to determine what the value would be if you did X, Y, and Z to the home. Let's assume X, Y, and Z will cost you $20,000 and that the home would be worth $100,000 once it's fixed up. Applying the ARV formula will tell you the maximum you should pay for this house in particular. Multiply ARV by 70 percent. Subtract the repair costs from your answer to see the maximum you're willing to pay for the home. In this case, that would be $100,000 x 70 percent = $70,000. $70,000 - $20,000 repair costs = $50,000. Therefore, the maximum you should be willing to pay for this one is $50,000.
  - What I look for in a rental: a minimum 1 percent rental rate per month of house purchase cost plus initial fix up. In other words, if I buy a house for $80,000, and it will cost me $20,000 to get it ready to rent, the lowest amount I'm willing to earn on rent is $1,000 a month.
- Want to learn more? My best recommendation for investing knowledge is the podcast *BiggerPockets.* They have some great books out now too, but just listening to their podcast will give you the knowledge you need.

5. Real estate success may mean pushing through a few lean years. Don't expect to hit it big when you first start out, no matter what your connections are. If there is one thing that real estate is really good at doing, it's humbling you. Expect some awful deals and some crazy, never-going-to-happen-again flukes that will test your resolve whether to get out of the business. Get ready for trouble and commit to pushing through it before it gets rough.

6. Go your own way. As you think through the best ways to grow your business and what you want to focus on, don't be afraid to believe

in yourself and take risks. Each new generation of real estate agents comes up with new ideas and approaches, and they are all worth trying. This business changes so fast that only one thing is certain: what worked for me, what worked for your broker, and what worked for your uncle who sold real estate thirty years ago will not be what works for you.

When I was first starting out, I had two generations of family already in the same business at my local office. I had some unique strengths that were very different from theirs, and there were times when it seemed as if we were in completely different businesses. In fact, the only reason my grandmother didn't try to talk me out of real estate after a couple of years was that my uncle believed my methods would pay off.

Don't be afraid to buck the trend and do something very different from what everyone else is doing. Often, that is exactly what it will take to make it in the real estate business.

Have you ever heard someone say that all you need for success is to follow your passion and success will come? Of course you have, probably more than once just this month. Unfortunately, it's bad advice.

Rather than following your passion and allowing success to follow, strive for success in a field where you have valuable skills. Success rarely follows passion, but passion almost always follows success.

This is good news for real estate agents because very few six-year-olds tell their parents that they want to sell real estate when they grow up. If you don't have a passion for real estate right now, don't worry about it. Real estate, like every other career, will be a lot more fun when you can build on small successes. Instead of worrying about whether you really like real estate, focus on skill acquisition and doing what it takes to get better at your job. Passion will follow.

I grew up wanting to be an entrepreneur and not really caring about which industry I would work in. It took me a while to find a groove in real estate and figure out if I could do it long-term. After doing the right things for years, I finally started to see my hard work pay off. When I realized that I could actually make a living in real estate, then my passion followed.

Now I have many different passions that I connect to the real estate business: helping others make smart financial decisions, growing long-term wealth, spending time with my family. Once you find some success in real estate, you will have the breathing room to define your *why* more clearly and to focus on the passion that will follow success. Now you have the basic building blocks for getting a head start. The next chapter will define the mindset you need as an agent.

Bonus Tip #1:

In real estate, the ability to bring your own actions and outlook in line with others is key. You must be attuned to your client's wants and needs right away, and you must establish rapport quickly to work with a client. One great way to do this is to assume that your client has all the power and knows more than you do. When we position ourselves arrogantly, we often overlook important details we should know about our client. Taking a position of humility and being open to learning from anyone you are working with is a great way to establish rapport.

Mindset of a Real Estate Agent

"We like to think of our champions and idols as superheroes who were born different from us. We don't like to think of them as relatively ordinary people who made themselves extraordinary."

—Carol Dweck

Energy vs. Time

Energy, not time, is the best way to gauge your effectiveness in life and in business. This may be even more true for real estate than anything else. You can work eighty-hour weeks as an agent and go nowhere fast. Break out of the per-hour mentality that we are spoon-fed starting in kindergarten. Instead of focusing on the time you have to put in, focus on the four areas you have to align to increase your energy potential. These areas are physical, emotional, mental, and spiritual. If you take a hard look at how to increase your effectiveness in each of these areas, your energy levels will skyrocket. So will your commissions.

Physical

While your purpose is the goal that will keep everything moving forward, your physical energy as a real estate agent is what will sustain your day-to-day action to accomplish your goals. Physical energy is often overlooked in books about improving real estate businesses. For that reason, there is more room to improve and to distance yourself from the competition if you can focus on increasing your physical energy.

There are three main areas you should concentrate on when it comes to physical energy: daily activity, diet, and sleep.

Daily Activity

As an agent, it's easy to let your daily activity level slip as you focus on making calls and sitting at the office instead of making your physical health a priority. Don't make this mistake. Richard Branson, mega entrepreneur and billionaire founder of Virgin, was asked to let people in on his best secret for success. His answer: "I definitely can achieve twice as much by keeping fit. It keeps the brain functioning well."[1]

Working out is an investment in your business that will pay huge dividends if you keep up with it consistently. Your physical health and activity level will affect every other area of your life, every day for the rest of your life. Taking the time to be fit should be a no-brainer. As a bonus, working out also provides many other benefits, including increasing your willpower if you can consistently keep up with it over time.

Don't make working out harder than it has to be. You don't have to run a marathon to get exercise. Here are some easy ways to increase your activity level with minimal effort:

1. Work out first thing in the morning if you can. An early win in the morning will improve your entire day.
2. Once you have a daily exercise regimen, concentrate on a routine that builds strength, like lifting weights. Strength takes a long time to build, but it also takes a long time to lose any gains. Sustained strength training is one of the best things you can do for long-term physical health.
3. Download the 7 Minute Workout app. This app delivers a seven-minute body workout to your phone every day. It's easy to commit to seven minutes and get it done.
4. Buy the book *Starting Strength* by Mark Rippetoe. There is no better book on lifting weights correctly. I also recommend *5/3/1*

by Jim Wendler for programming ideas once you are familiar with the basic lifts in *Starting Strength*.

5. Download an app for your weightlifting. I have used StrongLifts and an app called 531 Strength, but the important thing is to find one that works for you. Don't waste your willpower for the day figuring out what you want to do. Find a program you like, open your phone, and do it.

6. My routine right now is lifting weights four days a week, about ninety minutes each day. After lifting weights, I push a sled across a field a few times for cardio. On the off days, I try to play basketball or at least engage in some physical activity.

If you focus on your physical health and working out, you will get pushback from others who think you're wasting your time. Let them think that, and keep your focus on increasing your physical health. If you take the time to invest in your long-term health, you will grow your business.

Diet

Eating well is the second aspect of physical health you should concentrate on. Eating well is something we all know how to do, but few of us do it well. Don't make this harder than it has to be. Find ways to improve your diet. If you can make a small improvement each month, you'll be headed in the right direction.

Michael Pollan's advice from his book *In Defense of Food: An Eater's Manifesto* may be the best starting point: "Eat food. Mostly plants. Not too much." Commit to eating real food and not processed food. Work on eliminating sugar and white flour from your diet. Replace what you give up with plants, especially leafy greens.

The real secret to eating healthy is to eat exactly what you want to every day, but to change what you want. Changing what you want takes time, but you can actually change what kinds of foods you crave.

Our brains are wired for familiarity, and when your brain is used to popcorn, nachos, and ice cream (my old favorites), then that's what you will crave. If you can change your tastes to crave healthier foods, like nuts, salads, and roasted vegetables, then you will truly be able to eat what you want and get healthier at the same time.

The best way to get started on this path is to cut out sugar immediately. As soon as you do, find a leafy green you like and start eating more of it. I love arugula and have a salad almost every day. Don't neglect your diet when you're thinking about ways to invest in your business. If you don't eat right, you will have less energy throughout the day, poor physical health as you get older, and poor stamina. Eat better, live longer, and have more energy.

Sleep

The amount of sleep each person needs can vary, but it's an important part of maximizing your physical energy. Pay attention to the way you feel during the day and adjust your sleep patterns to improve. Here are some basic guidelines:

1. Get eight hours of sleep every night, no matter what.
2. Take a nap during the afternoon if you get tired. Naps are not a sign of laziness. A twenty-minute nap can significantly improve your productivity for the rest of your day. If you drag in the afternoon like most people, don't fight it. Close your eyes for a few minutes and finish your day strong.
3. Similarly, try a "nappuchino." The best naps last about twenty minutes. If you feel yourself getting tired, drink your favorite cup of coffee and then close your eyes. The caffeine will kick in to wake you up in about twenty minutes, and you will feel great.
4. Don't watch television right before bed.
5. Don't read nonfiction before bed. About two hours before I go to bed, I switch to fiction. Nonfiction engages the brain in too many ways to allow for good sleep.

6. Try skipping alcohol. I have found I sleep much better when I don't drink a glass of wine or two late at night.
7. Before bed, write out a simple plan for the following day, including what time to wake up.
8. Use a sleep mask. This could be the best ten bucks you ever spend. I estimate that I sleep an extra twenty to thirty minutes a night with a mask on, and those minutes add up quickly.
9. Get a good mattress. Don't be afraid to buy the best. You spend a third of your life in bed, so it makes sense to prioritize and buy the best mattress you can afford.

Increase your daily activity, improve your diet, and improve your sleep patterns. As agents, most of us want to find the quick fixes to increase our business or a secret software that a mega-agent is using to dominate. The real secret to success starts with having more physical energy and capacity than your competition so you can focus on all the other aspects of the business. Invest in yourself and start improving your physical health today.

Book Recommendations for Physical Energy

Good Calories, Bad Calories by Gary Taubes. This is a massive, extremely well-researched book. If you're looking for the definitive work on why we should avoid sugar and overprocessed flour, read this book.

Why We Get Fat by Gary Taubes. This is the simplified and shorter version of the above. It's easier to wade through quickly and about five hundred pages shorter than *Good Calories, Bad Calories*.

The 4-Hour Body by Timothy Ferriss. There is some really good stuff in here, including plans for a slow-carb (*slow*, not *low*) diet that's easy to follow and still yields results. A slow-carb diet is a great starting place for diet change. There is also advice on increasing your bench press, training for a marathon, and finding the best ab workouts.

Keto for Cancer by Miriam Kalamian. The ketogenic diet is a low-carb, high-fat diet that has some unique health benefits. This book shows how it can help battle cancer, but it's also a fascinating account on just how wrong most dietary advice is.

Starting Strength by Mark Rippetoe. I mentioned this above, but it's worth pointing out again. If you want to start strength training with barbells, you need this book. It's a great starting point to make sure you're lifting correctly and preserving your health.

Mindless Eating by Brian Wansink. This book focuses on the psychology of eating rather than dieting. It offers great advice and fascinating studies on why we eat what we eat and how to enjoy the right kinds of food even more. Want to eat less? Use a smaller plate.

Unconventional Medicine by Chris Kresser. This is a manifesto written for doctors and others in the medical field, but I found it very helpful as a layperson. It's an important critique of our modern healthcare system, and it emphasizes optimizing health every day rather than treating illness as it crops up.

Emotional

Of the four factors that we should focus on to increase energy, the emotional aspect of energy is easily the most overlooked. Most of us never think about our emotional energy until it is sapped from us on a daily basis and we have nowhere else to turn. Thinking through the kind of emotional support you need and the kind of negative energy you should avoid can be invaluable.

Have you noticed that real estate agents often have trouble with their family life? Whether it's work-life balance, divorce, or just never having enough time, real estate tends to expose emotional issues faster than many other industries. What can you do as an agent to ensure success while maintaining life-giving emotional support?

Partner for Life

There are many pieces of advice in this book that will help you grow your business and improve as a real estate agent. You can apply many of them right away and increase your business substantially. However, if you have a bad marriage, almost nothing else you do is going to matter until you find a way to mend your relationship. Having a supportive spouse is part of the foundation you need to succeed.

If you're single, you can certainly succeed in real estate. In fact, being single is a much better option than being married to someone who will be a drain on your energy. However, if you want to be married one day, then focus on getting married before anything else.

Having a life partner to share your story with is the best part of success. If you have any desire for companionship and marriage, make it a focus. This is especially true for men, in my experience. Stop playing video games during your off time and go on some dates to find a spouse whom you can love and live with for decades. It will be much easier to do the right thing every day when you're working for a family and not just supporting yourself.

Get married, but be careful whom you marry. Choose someone who is supportive and not a drain on your energy. Dietrich Bonhoeffer has a great quote about marriage that I always go back to: "It is not your love that sustains the marriage, but from now on, the marriage that sustains your love."[2] Choosing the wrong partner will be detrimental to your business and, much more importantly, your life.

If you're married and struggling in your marriage, find a way to make it better rather than ignoring it. Go to counseling, read some books together, and focus on ways to improve your communication. One of the best things you can do is find a church to get involved in. Start sharing life with other people in a community. Let others speak into your life and don't insulate yourself and your family.

In almost every case, divorce should be off the table. Divorce will not solve your problem; divorce is kicking a problem down the road to deal with again and again. Marriage is often about responsibility, and until you take responsibility for your choices, it will be hard to move forward.

Support

Selling real estate can be hard for the agent, but sometimes it's even harder for those who live with the agent. My wife had a steady job, and the idea that I was going to work in a business without ever getting a guaranteed income was a tough pill to swallow. We worked through some hard questions, but in the end we found ways to support each other and make real estate work for both of us.

Some are born entrepreneurs, some develop it over time, and some marry into entrepreneurship. Be patient with your spouse if he or she is not wired the same way, and be grateful you have the advantage of seeing work from another perspective.

Stay Positive

Staying positive in the face of repeated rejection and disappointment is one of the keys to staying afloat when real estate isn't going well. Remaining optimistic about tomorrow despite the bad outcomes of today is not easy, but it is one of the most important mindsets you can develop. You won't be able to control all the bad things that could happen to you in real estate, but you can control how fast you forget about them and move on.

Book Recommendations for Emotional Energy

Nonviolent Communication by Marshall Rosenberg. Get this one on Audible. It's the lecture given by Rosenberg, not the actual book.

The written book is a little convoluted, but the lecture gets his ideas across well. He has great ideas on how to communicate effectively without hurting others.

To Sell Is Human by Daniel H. Pink. Dan Pink has some great tools for staying positive in this book, especially for salespeople. If it is something you are struggling with, I highly recommend picking up a copy.

The Meaning of Marriage by Timothy Keller. Keller offers a great look at what marriage really means. It's worth picking up and studying whether you're single or already married.

On the Shortness of Life by Seneca. This is one I reread every year. It will help you gain perspective quickly and reorient where you need to go. Here's my favorite quote: "You act like mortals in all that you fear, and immortals in all that you desire."[3]

The Obstacle Is the Way by Ryan Holiday. Holiday offers principles of stoic philosophy applied to modern life. It's a great book to pick up and read a little bit at a time and will help you enjoy the struggle of getting to the finish line.

Mental
Increasing your mental energy is the third aspect of energy you should focus on. There are many ways to increase mental energy, but the best way is to be a lifelong learner. Don't assume you know enough or that there is nothing else useful out there for you. Few of us say we already know everything, but most of us act as if we do.

How many times have you heard, "I don't have time to read" or "I wish I had your job, then I would be able to read a lot more." Force yourself to not be one of those people. When you decide to do something else instead of learning, be honest with yourself. Never use "I don't have time" as an excuse. Instead, say, "Learning is not a priority for me today because I have [this] to do."

Imagine there are two agents, one who commits to learning and one who decides to wing it as long as he or she can. We'll call them the learning agent and the just-fine agent. The learning agent commits to reading two books a month that will help further his career. Conservatively, let's say that the agent picks up one tip a month he can use the rest of his life. That one tip could increase his business by just one half of 1 percent. Imagine that same agent five years down the road. How about twenty years? The agent who has committed to learning will be dramatically better off in almost every case.

Why should you read? David Osborne says that one of his mentors put it like this: "The greatest minds in human history have spent years condensing the best of what they know into a few pages that can be purchased for a few dollars, read in a few hours, and shorten your learning curve by decades. But I get it . . . . you're too busy."[4]

The reality is that you don't have time *not* to read. If you aren't reading, taking classes, and developing professionally, then you're falling behind. Here are a few strategies I use to learn:

- I read over a hundred books a year. There are many different ways to get this done, but keep in mind you don't have to read that many to make a difference. According to the Pew Research Center, the average college graduate reads (in whole or in part) seven books a year.[5] Even if you read just two books a month, you'll increase your knowledge base four times faster than the average.
- If you want to start reading more, here are some tips:
  ⊚ Read all the time. I carry books with me wherever I go.
  ⊚ Learn to listen to audiobooks. Driving in my truck is one of my favorite times to read.

- Read great books. Find sources that can recommend what you like.
- Read what you love. Don't worry about what you're reading at first; read anything you really love. I still love to read fiction and find it just as helpful as nonfiction.
- Find a group you can share with. I started a reading group that gets together once a month and talks about what they've read recently. The only rule is that we each have to read two books, any two books, a month.
- Want recommendations? I put out a monthly newsletter with all the books I read the previous month and a short review of each. Subscribe by sending me an email and asking to be added to the list: Brad@BeversRealEstate.com.

- Learn online. Sign up for classes on Udemy or CreativeLive. There are some really great courses online that will teach you how to analyze deals better, read body language, negotiate, and much more. Don't be afraid to spend money on your education. If you are in this for the long haul, it's one of the best investments you can make.
- Find a mentor or a coach. I use a business coach, and paying for his services is one of the best investments in my mental energy that I make. Having a coach that can keep you focused on the important, high-value areas in your business is invaluable.

Book Recommendations for Mental Energy

The 4-Hour Workweek by Timothy Ferriss. This is still one of my favorite business books. It's helped shape my business more than any other book. The title is deceiving, but the content is great. Thinking smarter may help you more than working harder.

The First 20 Hours by Josh Kaufman. Kaufman offers great examples on how to learn things very quickly by breaking them down. It's a good read with some brilliant ideas on learning fast.

Miracle Morning Millionaires by Hal Elrod and David Osborne. Putting a morning routine in place that actually works will help you get a crazy amount of work done every day. My morning routine frees me up for the rest of the day so that I can concentrate on professional development.

Eat That Frog! by Brian Tracy. This is one of my favorite books on short, very practical ways to get things done quickly. Use this to end procrastination and free up more time.

Mindhacker by Ron Hale-Evans and Marty Hale-Evans. This book covers a wide variety of topics, but the advice on reading changed the way I read books. Some of the best tips that I frequently use include reading with a multi-pen handy for notes, creating my own index system for marking in books, and creating a personalized index and table of contents for the material I like best in a book.

Spiritual

The spiritual dimension of energy is recognizing what your true purpose in life and business is, then centering your efforts and energy on that purpose. Take a minute to think about why you want to sell real estate and what it means to you. Really think about it for just a moment.

What's your answer? Is it enough to carry you through the hard times? There will be hard times. Here are some ways to help define and deepen your purpose so that you will have the energy to push through and keep going. The spiritual dimension of energy will be the engine that drives everything else.

The Tombstone Test

In 1981, the year before I was born, my grandparents opened the real estate company I now own. I had the unique privilege of working every day with them. My grandmother was my broker, the only broker I ever worked under. For fifteen years, I learned by watching her conduct business and interact with people.

In 2018, she passed away after battling with cancer. This was a hard time for our family, but we were also comforted by knowing she was ready to go and had a foundation of rock-solid faith. I had admired her impact in the community for a long time, but going to her funeral was still an eye-opening experience for me. Multiple clients gave eulogies on how she had changed their lives. Many of our agents did the same. There were even agents from other companies who spoke of her impact on their lives. My grandmother was a gifted real estate agent and broker, a saleswoman who really knew her business. But she always put people first, and that's what she's remembered for.

What do you want to be remembered for? One of the first assignments from my business coach was the Tombstone Test. Imagine that you have died, and your tombstone is being engraved. What would you want it to say? Pull out a blank piece of paper and draw a tombstone on it. Put your name and birthdate on the tombstone, then add what you would like it to say underneath when you are gone.

Defining Your Values and Vision

One of the most helpful tasks you can work on as a business owner is to define your core values, purpose, and long-term vision. First, define your core values. These are the principles essential to your business—so essential that if any of them were missing, even just one, you couldn't sell real estate any longer. You should have three to five core values that define what really drives your business—values you won't compromise on. Here are my personal core values for my own business:

1. My clients are always #1.
2. I will always encourage entrepreneurship.
3. I will help my agents succeed.
4. I will love real estate and all that comes with it.

What are your core values?

You should come up with three to five core values. Remember, if you can continue in your work as an agent with one of those core values missing, then it was not a core value to begin with. When you first come up with the core values, they will likely be longer than my examples above. That is normal. Revisit them once a week and keep trying to distill them into smaller chunks. You will find that over time you can make them more succinct.

Purpose

After you determine your core values, think about your defining purpose. How can you sum up your purpose in a single sentence to a client? Keep your core values within the company, but share your purpose with the client. What is the purpose that keeps you going through the hard times?

Hint: your purpose should have nothing to do with money. Making money and increasing your commissions is a fine goal, but it should never be your purpose. Your purpose should point to something larger. Here is my purpose statement:

To help clients make one of the biggest decisions of their lives and love the choice that they make. We do anything it takes to build confidence and prove that we can be trusted.

Think about your own purpose statement as it relates to real estate. What would success look like? How would you be able to help your clients? How about your community?

Vision

Finally, think about your vision for the future. How many years do you want to be in real estate? Fifty years from now, what will people think when they hear your name? Your vision should be personal and summed up in a paragraph or two. Think about your legacy, your long-term impact, and where you want the business to be in ten, twenty, and fifty years. Here is a sample vision:

We will be known for our outstanding reputation and a mindset always favoring relationships over individual sales. We will be a place where like-minded entrepreneurs can grow a business quickly and see their hard work pay off. We will be known as problem solvers, never exhausting ideas to help our clients realize their dreams of owning a property. Fifty years from now, our company will still be known for honesty, hard work, and creativity. Our name will mean creative technology, business savvy, and long-term relational sales, no matter what.

What Will Your Vision for Your Own Business Be?

The most important part of sustaining enough energy is spirituality. Unless you have a strong underlying purpose, you will not have the energy to do anything else. And frankly, it won't matter in the long run. If you aren't ready to nail down what your driving purpose is, that is not unusual. Try putting the first things down that come to your mind in this section right now and plan to revisit them in six months. As you grow, you will keep refining your vision and purpose until they are crystal clear.

Bonus Tip #2

One of the best things I ever did for my business was hire a business coach. At our first meeting, the free one that I agreed to so I could get a nice lunch, I told the coach that this would probably be the last time we would meet. I believed there wasn't much a coach could bring to the table for me. I was already a dedicated self-learner growing at a steady pace.

I haven't missed a coaching session since that day almost seven years ago. The value of a coach for a real estate agent is impossible to overestimate. Here is what it has done for me:

- *Helped me to work on my business rather than in my business. Continually thinking about the right things and having someone looking over my shoulder is an enormous benefit.*
- *I estimate that I get big things done 30 percent faster with a coach. I would do them anyway, but using a coach gets them done faster. You may not think that's a big deal, but one example of doing something faster is publishing my first book. I probably published six months earlier than I would have without a coach, which was easily worth six figures for my business.*
- *You are alone when you're building your business. Having someone give you a fresh perspective is invaluable.*
- *It's a business deduction on your taxes. Hiring a coach, if you are serious about being a successful agent, should be an easy decision.*

Taking the Long View

One of the best advantages you can have as a real estate agent comes from committing to the business long term. If you have a long-term view, you'll think about marketing and sales very differently from an agent who is just after a quick commission or two. Many agents dream of using real estate as a springboard to other businesses. Instead, if you commit to thinking like an agent who will be around for decades, you can beat the competition over time.

Here are just some of the advantages of taking the long view:

- Paying for leads from Zillow and similar sites becomes much more valuable. When I buy leads for buyers, I always tell myself that I'm really buying listings five or ten years from now. Once you have a buyer you've sold a property to, you have your foot in the door to list the property next time.
- Ethical and moral questions become very easy to answer. If you're in this business for a long time, doing the right thing will become automatic. You will make more money in the long run by doing the right thing.
- You will build up a good relationship with many different agents. This is very important when it comes to future deals. You'll know how other agents think, and you can take advantage of it in unique ways.
- The real estate business is like rolling a giant snowball. It takes a long time to get going, but once you pick up speed, you'll be

impossible to stop. Commit to the long term, and you'll reap the rewards after you have put in the work.

- Repeat clients are very lucrative if you take good care of them. One of my best clients has never bought a property over $200,000, but she has bought and sold eight of them with me. From her commissions as well as the buyers that I landed by listing the properties, she's been one of my best clients. She's also made a lot of money going on this real estate journey with me. Taking the long view, you treat all clients as if they are one of your best—and often they will be.

- Be a systems agent more than an outcomes agent. Rather than focus on the outcome of any one transaction, focus on the fact that if you do the right things over and over again, your business will grow. There will be flukes: you can sell some big properties while you're doing everything wrong, and you can fail over and over while doing the right things. The important principle to remember is to keep pushing forward with the system, and the outcomes will line up. Judge yourself not on the sale or the commission, but on whether you stuck with the system and did the right things to make it happen.

Bonus Tip #3:

Don't be arrogant and expect things to come easily—they won't. There will be times when you'll want to quit, but stick with it. You started down this path for a reason, and you have to push through the hard parts to reap the rewards.

There are other jobs and careers out there, but your potential in real estate is literally unlimited. You can do anything you want to do and be as successful as you desire to be if you do the right things. Keep at it.

Everyone Is Selling Something

The skills needed for salesmanship are now required for more and more jobs, and that will only increase in the future. No matter what career you choose, you'll have to sell something, whether you're an employee selling the need for a raise to your boss, a mom selling your kids on eating broccoli, or a nonprofit selling your work.

What does that mean for agents? First, 100 percent of your time is sales. Since you're working on a commission basis, everything you do should be considered sales—prospecting, marketing, networking, writing a contract, or even reading a book on real estate. You can use your time in real estate to become an expert salesperson, and that will benefit any future endeavor.

"Nothing happens until someone sells something." Many people have said this over and over again, but I remember hearing it for the first time from my grandad. His point was that nothing happens in any economy until you convince someone to change.

As an industry, real estate enjoyed a special advantage for decades that at one time seemed impossible to overcome. We agents had all of the information, and we were the distributors of secret knowledge that very few others were able to grasp. In industries across the board, real estate included, the internet has created an information parity that has all but eliminated that knowledge gap.

Your clients can figure out anything they want to know. If they really wanted to, they could find contracts online, figure out which title company to use, and even contact sellers directly. They are no longer stuck using whomever they meet first. Now they have the tools to evaluate agents online and learn about the process of real estate like never before.

In fact, clients will often know more about the properties you're looking at than you do. I've had clients who literally knew the last two hundred years of ownership history not only on the properties we saw, but also on all the properties surrounding it. They know where the sellers work, how long they've owned it, whether they're local or not, and much more. As an agent in the brave new world, don't fight this. Your clients will often be better informed than you.

In a world of information parity, what advantage does a real estate agent have? Why should a client still use a real estate agent when she can find much of the information on her own? Daniel H. Pink, author of *To Sell Is Human*, sums up much of his thinking by pointing out that the old adage *caveat emptor* (buyer beware) has now shifted to *caveat venditor* (seller beware, or in our case, agent beware).

In the past, buyers were warned about shady salesmen and had to take extra precautions because, well, buyer beware. With information parity, the opposite is becoming more and more true. If you burn a client once, it is likely that everyone will know about it. You must always provide outstanding service that deserves good reviews, or you'll be fighting a losing battle before you even meet with a new client.

Assume your prospects and clients have more information than you have or can easily obtain it. What is your role in a property transaction and how can you offer unique value to your clients, keeping in mind this new paradigm?

First, sending properties to your buyers should be the least of what you do. This may have been the whole game a few years ago, but now it's rare for you to know about a property before clients know about it. You should still send them options and give inside knowledge when you have it, but this is simply the baseline and should in no way be considered a plan to grow your business.

Remember that from a client's point of view, you are a salesperson working on commission; you have a financial incentive for selling them something as expensive as possible as quickly as you can. You should take extra care not to push one particular property over another. Instead of thinking of yourself as an agent who sells properties, think of yourself as an agent who sells professional property-consulting services to clients. My goal in every showing is not to sell one particular home or property, but to sell myself as the best agent to help the client make the best purchase.

Don't shy away from being in sales. Everyone sells something, and you'll get better training in sales than everyone else because you'll be doing it each day. Just remember you are selling your services much more often than any particular home or property.

Introverts vs. Extroverts

When you think of salespeople, who do you think of? Pause for a minute and reflect on who comes to mind. What do salespeople look like? How do they speak? What social circles do they run in? Are they introverted or extroverted?

For most of us, the prototypical salesperson is a man in a suit, maybe selling cars, and definitely extroverted. That's the American image that has been ingrained into our culture through books and television and continuously supported by our own experience.

But it's not exactly true. The truth is that extroverts can be very good at sales, but introverts and ambiverts (those between the two extremes) have unique advantages as well. If you aren't the typical extrovert, don't worry. You have built-in advantages the extroverts don't, and you need to take advantage of them. Most people are neither introverted nor extroverted, but fall on the scale between. Here are some of the advantages of being "in the middle."

Advantages of the Ambivert

- Ambiverts are flexible, able to adapt to different types of clients. They can fit into different situations more easily. If they have to talk and socialize, they can—even if it's for a limited time.
- They know when to stay quiet. Plato said it this way: "Wise men speak because they have something to say; fools because they have to say something."[1]
- The truth is that sometimes the best thing you can do is just listen and shut up. For many extreme extroverts, that can be nearly impossible.
- They are willing to learn. Extroverts tend to be overconfident in their own skill set and knowledge base; therefore, they concentrate much less on learning new things. Just by reading this book and dedicating yourself to learning, you are showing your flexibility.
- Ambiverts are patient, tending to take the longer view more often when dealing with clients. They can see that the immediate sale is dwarfed by the importance of a long-term relationship with the client.

I am definitely not an extrovert. I fall on the ambivert scale but closer to the introvert side. There is no doubt that being more introverted than extroverted has been a challenge at times, but overall I think it's been very good for my business. If you're an introvert, know that there is a path to success for you. In fact, if you can stay with it for the long haul, there's a good chance you can outpace most extroverts.

Pick up a copy of *The Introvert's Edge: How the Quiet and Shy Can Outsell Anyone* by Matthew Pollard if you want to learn how to maximize your natural advantages as an introvert or ambivert. Or, if you are definitely an extrovert, this will help you strengthen areas you may be weak in.

Bonus Tip #4:

I hate virtual tours. If you've shown property for any length of time, you know that when clients walk into a home, they immediately have an emotional reaction. That emotion is impossible to replicate in a virtual tour.

The listing online should not have absolutely everything you could ever want to see on the property. Instead, it should entice the buyer to come look at it themselves.

Showing properties live will also give you a chance to connect with clients in person, build rapport, and show them the best features of the house while answering any concerns or objections promptly. Putting a virtual tour online and letting people click through will mean fewer property showings and is a disservice to the property owners you're working with.

The 80/20 Agent

The 80/20 rule is one of the most important principles to remember when you start your career. It's a rule that seems to govern almost everything in the universe. First discovered by an Italian mathematician named Pareto, it is sometimes called the Pareto Principle. The rule states that 80 percent of any outcome results from 20 percent of the input. Applied to real estate, the rule means this: 80 percent of commissions come from 20 percent of the clients. 80 percent of commissions are earned by 20 percent of the agents. 80 percent of your own income results from 20 percent of your work.

Think about your local market and the real estate company where you work, and you'll quickly realize how true this rule is. There are a few agents at the top who seem to collect the bulk of commissions while everyone else struggles to get by. You can choose to be overrun by the 80/20 rule, or you can choose to be a part of the 20 percent.

Before you ignore this rule, do the math. If you're in the 20 percent who reaps the 80 percent results, you're making sixteen times more commissions than someone in the 80 percent. That's the difference between struggling and flourishing. When you start out as an agent, don't plan to be average. Average agents will never turn real estate into a career. It will just be a job, and a low-paying one to boot. Instead, shoot for the 20 percent, and you'll reap many rewards once you get to the top.

How do you get to the 20 percent? Is it as simple as wanting it? There are a few things you can do to help ensure you get there as soon as possible.

1. Be patient. Don't try to reach the 20 percent in your first three months as a real estate agent. Real estate can be very discouraging when viewed in the short term, and I've seen agents burn out quickly. Set your long-term goal and follow the action steps that it will take to get to the top.

2. Become an expert. The first step toward being a top agent is having real expertise. This should be a baseline for all agents, but unfortunately it's not. If you haven't realized it yet, the real estate field is not made up of Mensa scholars and child prodigies. The majority of agents never take the time to know their field really well.

3. Practice contracts with your broker, take extra classes, read every single day, take online courses, and build up a knowledge base that will be very hard for others to overcome. It's not that hard if you work on it every day. The average agent wants the rewards without the work, wanting to be in the 20 percent without laying a solid foundation.

4. Stand out. One of the best books you can read on marketing is *The 22 Immutable Laws of Marketing* by Al Ries and Jack Trout. The most important principle you learn is that it's always better to be the first, no matter what. Figure out what niche in real estate you can claim to be first in, just in your local market, and you'll dominate. It will be very difficult for anyone to catch up to you. For instance, I'm the first agent in my market to write a book (*Texas Farm & Ranch Guide*).

5. Partner with a popular nonprofit group and give 10 percent of your commissions toward it. This turns you into a philanthropist, not a salesman.

6. Write a book and be an expert. I took this route, and it has paid off. Writing a book is not as hard as it sounds, especially with the tools in place today.

7. Own a neighborhood. If there is a small neighborhood over-looked by other agents, own it. Give everyone in the neighborhood a small gift every month or two; introduce yourself by knocking on doors; send mailers out. Learn everything there is to know about it. If you do this enough, it will be hard for anyone living there to list with anyone else.
8. Host a big party for the community. Free beer and barbecue still work when you want to build your network quickly.
9. Get involved. Don't spend all your free time with other real estate agents. Get involved with real people, minister to your church, serve nonprofits, volunteer at food banks, and join an historical society. One of the best things about being an agent is that meeting and serving others is a part of your job.
10. Visualize success. When it seems like reaching the 20 percent is an impossible goal, ask yourself what it will feel like to finally reach that point. How will it feel to be at the very top, to not have to work so hard, to be known as an expert, to have clients come to you and not have to negotiate your commission down? Ask yourself what your life could be like five years from now, and then visualize it. This practice teaches your brain where you want to go, and the action steps to get there will become more clear if you continue this practice daily.
11. Market in the right way. Many business owners and agents throw money at marketing like they're throwing beads at pretty girls in a Mardi Gras parade. Don't buy into the shotgun marketing approach. There are specific steps you must take to create effective marketing, and they're not that expensive. Buy marketing books by Dan Kennedy and start studying.
    - Think of yourself as a marketer who happens to sell real estate, not as a real estate agent who needs to market every once in a while. Everyone is in the marketing business, whether he or she likes it or not. Be the best marketer, and reaching the 20 percent will happen faster than you think.

- One of the worst mistakes agents make when they market is neglecting to find out where their leads are coming from. Often, agents will ask clients what brought them in or made them call. If you have to ask, then you're not doing it right.
- Every piece of marketing you have out there should implement a specific call to action with a unique ask. When that call to action is triggered, you know which marketing campaign has succeeded and when it happens. Here are some examples of things to think through when you are deciding how to market:
  - ◉ Don't waste your business card: include a call to action. At the bottom of my card, I have a free offer for my book, *Texas Farm & Ranch Guide*. If someone calls or emails and says they want to take advantage of the offer they found on the business card, I know it worked.
  - ◉ Create value with simple reports. One of my favorite marketing tools is setting up a system in which prospects can request something simple, like a free report on investing in land. If you create something very specific, then start pushing it out there, you will see who's interested very quickly.
  - ◉ Unique call to actions are key. You can set these up in a number of ways, and once you start working on them you'll think of many more. You could have the same report but title it differently for each campaign. You could set up different phone numbers or emails depending on the campaign. Never market without a call to action, or you're just wasting your hard-earned money with no way to measure whether it works.
  - ◉ Use A/B testing to constantly improve. When you land on a marketing idea, use the power of A/B testing to see what's more effective. For example, offer a report with a certain title to the first half of your mailing list alphabetically, and offer a different title to the second half. When people ask about it,

you'll immediately know which report they received. Some titles clearly outperform others, and you can improve your next campaign using this information.

12. Follow up. This is boring, but it's also a reason many real estate agents fail. Look around your local market and see who the most successful agents are. The agents selling the most property usually have a very simple secret that I'm about to share with you: they follow up with their clients and prospects.

That's it. Sometimes, following up is all it takes to move from failure to success, and it's as simple as regularly contacting the people you've already been talking with. Remember that when someone talks to you as an agent, he's probably already talked to a couple of other agents as well. You're in a race to see who will win his business, and if you follow up more frequently and with better information, then you're way ahead of the game.

One time, I received an email asking about a large listing we had at the time, over six hundred acres. I followed up and answered the questions the client had, but never heard back. I decided it was worth following up anyway, and at least once every two weeks I sent an email (that was the only contact information I had) and asked if I could provide any more information or if I could deliver it in person.

Almost a year later, he finally responded and said that if the property was still on the market, he'd like to see it. He was selling another property and ready to buy. I showed him this one property, and he purchased it to flip, so I had it listed again a year later. This one instance of following up has meant over twelve million dollars in sales for my business so far.

You won't always have clients looking at the larger, more expensive properties, but the principle of following up remains the same. I love following up, even when I sense that the clients or prospects are getting annoyed with how often I contact them. My rule is that they either have to respond positively, or they have to ask me to stop. Ignoring me won't work.

Other agents have asked me about the dangers of being too annoying and driving someone away, but that's a remote possibility. People really appreciate when you stay on top of things and don't let things slide. Following up consistently also shows your clients how you'll market their listing or how you'll work for them as buyers.

Following up is probably the simplest thing you can do, especially if you invest in a good customer relationship management software (I use Contactually). But it is one of the most effective. In fact, if you wanted to do just one thing on this list for the highest return, follow up. It costs you nothing, and the returns will be enormous over time.

Bonus Tip #5:

Don't waste your time with other real estate agents. Spend time with those in your office but avoid other agents. You should seek out a mentor or two, and once you're established, you should seek out others to mentor. But don't spend time with other real estate agents outside of your immediate sphere of influence. There is a temptation to seek approval, commiserate with, and seek rewards from other agents, but you should avoid it at all costs.

Instead of spending your time going to agent happy hours, board meetings, and get-togethers, join an organization where you will meet clients and interact with real people. Always remember the 80/20 rule for agents: 20 percent of the agents make 80 percent of sales. When you spend time with the 80 percent, you're dragging yourself down.

First Impressions

As a real estate agent, you need to make a good first impression very quickly. Here are some things you can do to stand out from the competition and establish rapport right away.

First, when you initially meet someone, make sure you give him or her a firm handshake. This is Sales 101, but I'm still surprised at how many people have a truly bad handshake. Word of warning: if I shake your hand and it's weak, I will have an unfavorable impression of you for the rest of our time together.

Your clients will be the same way. The practice of shaking hands likely came from warriors showing their hands to be empty and proving they were not holding any weapons. When you approach someone, have your hands out of your pockets and offer to shake his or her hand and do it firmly.

Second, develop your own questions to ask your client at your first meeting. Often when I meet someone for the first time, I'm also about to jump in a car or truck with him to go look at some property for a few hours. There is nothing worse than being in a car with a client and running out of things to say. Fortunately, there are ways to prevent this from happening to you, ever.

Work on memorizing a few key questions and use them to learn more about your clients as you drive around. Asking questions they don't often hear will cause them to think through their answers more carefully and also to remember you. When we have unique or unusual conversations, there is a stronger chance for connection. Vanessa Van Edwards gives examples of some of these questions that she calls conversation sparkers in her excellent book *Captivate*:

- Working on any exciting projects lately?
- What was the highlight of your day?
- Working on any personal passion projects?
- Have any vacations coming up? (I love this one.)
- What's your story?
- What are you up to this weekend?
- What do you do to unwind?[1]

You can easily come up with questions that aren't hard to answer and aren't cliché either. Some of my personal favorite questions that open up conversations quickly are the following:

- Will this be a weekend place, or are you looking for something full-time?
- How many kids do you have? (I have four, so this is a good point of connection; people love talking about their children.)
- Any thoughts on what kind of schools you would be interested in here? (I love to talk about education with people, so this is a good way to open up a topic you can talk about for a while.)

Another way to stand out is by making sure you stand out in their memory. Here are a few things you can do to make sure this happens:

- Put an unusual quote on your business card or email signature.
- Send a thank-you gift after meeting someone rather than just a card.

- Think through what your office offers people when they first come in. Would it be more effective to offer coffee and water like everyone else? What if you could offer espresso, fresh-squeezed lemonade, or even hot chocolate?

Finally, work out a plan that details the questions you're going to ask and stories you're going to tell before each interaction with a client. Think through the different traits you want your clients to pick up on, and be prepared to use them. Traits you want to convey could include these:

- Unique expertise in your area
- Negotiation expertise
- Community expert
- What your values are—family, church, charity
- Why your area is better than the other areas they've looked at

These simple things will help you stand out from the other agents your client is bound to meet. Make sure you have a firm handshake, have questions ready to keep the conversation moving, and stand out as memorable.

Bonus Tip #6:

You will sell real estate a lot faster if you don't wear flip-flops. The old saying "Fake it 'til you make it" is a cliché because it's true. Here's how to dress for success:

- *Dress as close to your ideal client as possible. Don't wear a suit if you sell ranches, and don't wear boots and jeans if you sell commercial real estate.*

- *Avoid facial hair if possible. First impressions are everything, and studies continue to show that men with facial hair are viewed as less trustworthy than those without.*
- *Get a haircut regularly. Look sharp.*
- *Iron your shirts even if your attire is closer to casual than formal.*
- *Remember that you are new to the business. I was twenty-two when I started, and one of the decisions I made was to wear glasses instead of contacts. It made me look older, and every little bit helps.*
- *Dress nicer than usual for closings. It is a special occasion, and by dressing nicer, you are showing your clients you are a professional.*

It's All Your Fault

One mindset that holds new agents back is the inability to accept responsibility for what happens to them. As an agent, you will lay everything on the line at times in order to win a listing or secure a sale. Sometimes you will fail. And it will be all your fault.

Don't take the sting out of failure by blaming others. I can't tell you how many times I've heard, "I would have won the listing, but they decided to go with their friend." Or, "That's the way it goes—win some, lose some." If you lost and another agent won, you need to accept responsibility for what happened and change before your next appointment. Maybe you didn't know enough, maybe your social skills need to improve, or maybe you need to bring in a partner for this type of listing next time.

Whatever happens, use a critical eye and be ruthless with yourself. Accepting responsibility is the only way you will improve. If you blame others or outside circumstances, there is no reason for you to change. It was not your fault anyway.

This is a lesson my grandmother instilled in me when I started real estate. One of the first clients I worked with was looking for some acreage on which to build a weekend house. We saw a few places and finally narrowed it down to a great listing our company had—forty acres with spectacular views on a country road.

I was twenty-two and about to make my largest sale so far, so I was excited. They wanted to sleep on it and decide what to offer, so we parted ways and promised to talk the next day. When I hadn't heard from them by the afternoon, I called but didn't get an answer. After calling again later with no response, I sent an email the following day.

They finally got back to me. The good news was that they were going to make an offer on the property. The bad news was that they weren't going to use me. They had decided to use an agent outside of our office because we had the listing. They had already signed a buyer's representation agreement with the other agent and an offer would be coming in soon.

Embarrassed, I explained what had happened to my grandmother. She reminded me that real estate is never easy and that this could be a learning moment, or I could ignore it. It would be easy to ignore it. After all, how could I help what had happened? They were obviously disloyal buyers who couldn't be trusted anyway. Good riddance.

Fortunately, I chose to accept responsibility. My grandmother's knowing look as she laid out the options definitely helped push me in the right direction. Here are some of the lessons I learned from this teachable moment:

1. I failed to make myself invaluable to a client. As a real estate agent, you should make your value so clear right off the bat that it is impossible for the client to imagine using anyone else.
2. I failed to use a proper closing technique to write up an offer that day. Even if we had just started writing an offer together so they could take it home and think about it, it would have cemented me as their agent.
3. I failed to properly explain the brokerage relationship. This is something confusing for buyers and sellers alike, and if you just provide the minimum disclosures required by law, it won't be enough. Take the time to carefully explain what it means in layman's terms.

4. I failed to have a complete knowledge base that I could use with clients. Since that time, I have learned hundreds of things you need to know about raw land in the country. Knowing and sharing some of those at this early stage would have secured the sale for me.

5. I failed to establish enough rapport with the client. I didn't know, and didn't use, some of the rapport-building techniques I will share in this book. Giving a gift, sharing client testimonials, or even just asking more questions about their lives would have gone a long way.

One sale, one mistake, but lasting consequences. That same property has since sold a couple more times. I lost tens of thousands of dollars in commissions because I didn't accelerate my learning curve and take responsibility before it happened. You will fail as a real estate agent; you will be embarrassed; you will have your pride hurt. Don't waste the opportunity by ignoring it. Use it.

Bonus Tip #7:

The ability to face failure and disappointment head-on and still stay afloat is a valuable trait for an agent. You need this ability in any sales job, but being an agent seems to take a special kind of resiliency. If you haven't had a deal fall through at the eleventh hour or been burned by an unscrupulous agent, you will.

When failures happen, always remind yourself that it won't last and it's not universal. Internalizing failures and thinking that failures are part of your identity will really hurt your business in the long run. You will create a self-fulfilling prophecy and end up with many more failures and lost deals when you can't find a way to stay resilient.

Goals, Habits,
and Following Through

*"Whenever you want to achieve something, keep your eyes open,
concentrate and make sure you know exactly what it is you want.
No one can hit their target with their eyes closed."*
—Paulo Coelho

Scheduling for Success

Real estate is a job in which you have to work seven days a week when the market is booming and adjust quickly when it's not. Having a consistent calendar and schedule is the best way to keep up with what you need to do and how to make things happen. Below are some things I do yearly, quarterly, monthly, and daily to accomplish what's needed.

Annual

I rely on setting goals and striving to meet them. One of my favorite things to do in December is to look back on my goals for the year, assess the results, and set goals for the next year. Through working with a business coach, I've learned a few things about goals that make them more effective:

1. Set SMART goals. Each goal you set should be:
   a. Specific. Set a specific target such as "making $100,000 a year," not just "making more money."
   b. Measurable. Make sure it's something you can measure. Don't set a goal to make twenty clients happy, because happiness is hard to measure. Set a goal to get twenty five-star reviews from clients.
   c. Achievable. Stretch goals are awesome, but don't set them so far out that they are demotivating. For your first year

in real estate, your goal should not be to take home five million.

    d. Relevant. Make sure your goals actually point to something you want to achieve. For instance, some agents track who mentions their billboard to them. If your goal is to be mentioned, then it worked. But if it is to get listings, then who cares how many people mention you?

    e. Time-bound. We are talking about annual goals here, but all your goals should be time-bound. Don't leave them open-ended.

2. Set RPA goals. In addition to SMART, your goals should always have the following:

    a. Result: what success will look like when you're finished.

    b. Purpose: why it's an important goal. What does getting ten listings really mean for your business?

    c. Action: thinking through the actions needed to reach your goal. These are broad strokes. You don't need to list every action. Categorize what you will do to help you keep your goals in mind and eventually accomplish them. These big actions can be broken into smaller chunks for quarters, months, weeks, and days as you start to make progress on your goals.

3. Don't just set business goals. Many of the examples I've used are business goals, but it's important to set goals in all areas of your life. This classic framework includes many different areas to focus on:

    a. Physical Environment

    b. Business/Career

    c. Finances

    d. Health

    e. Spiritual

    f. Family and Friends

g. Romance
h. Personal Growth
i. Fun and Recreation
j. Optional: Travel Goals (You should customize your goals and think about what is important to you.)

I highly recommend setting these goals—especially your annual goals—with someone who will keep you accountable. Your first choice should be a business coach, but if you aren't ready to take that step, find another agent or talk to your broker about setting some goals.

I also choose an annual focus or a single word to center on for the year. For example, I might focus on marketing, automation, habits, or writing. If there is one area that many of your annual goals seem to be targeted toward, choose a word that encompasses them.

Quarterly

Breaking down the annual goals into quarterly action steps is a good way to measure your progress throughout the year. At the beginning of each quarter, look at your annual goals and choose action steps to reach your goals. I recommend taking two or three days each quarter just to focus on your business. This quarterly retreat has been one of the most rewarding times for my business. I'm able to get a lot done when I can truly focus on the big picture for a couple of days each quarter. If you are able, go somewhere besides your home, or even your community. Change your environment and try to jar some new ideas loose.

Taking regular breaks from your normal routine will help you rise above and see what really needs to be focused on next. Keeping my head down and pushing through the hard work without taking regular time to reevaluate is one of the biggest mistakes I made early on. I kept pushing forward without taking time to assess my progress and direction.

Monthly

Break down your larger goals by monthly targets in addition to your quarterly goals. At the beginning of the month, figure out where you would like to be by the end of that month, and write it down.

For areas of annual focus, I will often draft a monthly plan at the beginning of the year. This is a nice way to make sure you hit all the highlights throughout the year without taking much brain space trying to figure out what to do next. For example, in the year I focused on marketing, January was the month I built our physical mailing list, February the month I learned how to make my own pay-per-click ads, March the month I mailed more books to property owners, and so on.

Weekly

Each week, I set targets for at least three big projects and think about what I need to get done for the rest of the week. The best planner I've found for planning my days and weeks is the Panda Planner. It's an undated monthly, weekly, and daily planner that will last you about six months. The layout is extremely helpful for converting monthly and weekly goals into daily targets.

What are the tasks you want to accomplish every week no matter what? For me, that includes finishing at least two books. Have a place where you can track these goals regularly and work on making them habits instead of goals. A goal is something that will take mental willpower to accomplish, while a habit should happen automatically with no extra effort on your part.

Daily

Having a consistent daily routine is vital in any business, but especially so in real estate. Real estate is often hard to predict, and you have to be willing to adjust on the fly. Because of that, it's extremely important to get the work that has to be done every day finished before anything else gets started. Waking up early and knocking out the things you have to do before anyone else is even awake is the best way to keep your day as flexible as possible for whatever may come.

To be successfully self-employed, it's important to develop your discipline and willpower. The more you stay true to your commitments and match your actions with your intents, the easier it will be to repeat those actions tomorrow. When an agent asks me the most important habit to implement to build a business, my answer is always, "Wake up early."

There are many benefits to waking up early and starting the day strong. It will improve every other part of your day. I know many agents already do this and have their own routine, but I will share my own schedule. I don't follow this every day, but I notice a huge difference when I'm able to stick with it.

Wake-Up
1. Commit to your morning wake-up time before you go to bed.
2. Wake up at 4:55 a.m. without snoozing the alarm.
3. Brush your teeth. (It helps you wake up faster.)
4. Drink a full glass of water. (You're dehydrated in the morning, and water helps to wake you up and reset your healthy hydration.)
5. Either shower or exercise, depending on the time you'll work out that day.

First Things
As you implement your new morning routine, remember SAVERS:

a. Silence: This includes prayer and meditation for me. I was born into a Christian family and have prayed most of my life, but this daily practice has changed how I pray for the better. Each morning I spend fifteen to twenty minutes in silence, and it continues to grow longer. Praying for others and for what God is doing will help you to recognize answered prayers and blessings as they come, rather than taking them for granted.

I am also working on meditation. After a few false starts over the years, I've found that using the app Headspace is a great solution for me. The ten-day training is free, so you can see if it is a fit for you. For me, meditation is a way to practice directing my thoughts where I want them to go. It's also one of the only ways to increase your willpower, and I love gaining more willpower each day.

b. Affirmations: I mentally review all my yearly goals in different areas, including health, business, reading, and family.

c. Visualization: I take time to imagine reaching those goals and what reaching those goals, especially the most important ones, will look like.

d. Exercise: If I don't work out that day or if I exercise in the afternoon, I still do push-ups or jumping jacks quickly in the morning to help get my blood flowing.

e. Reading: I read a lot during the day, but in the morning I listen to the *ESV: Through the Bible in a Year* podcast. There is an Old Testament, Psalms, and New Testament reading each day. I listen while I make my coffee. If you don't have a habit of reading, I would also use this time to read at least five pages of a business development book.

f. Scribing: I journal and plan for the day. I actually use three different planners each day, and all three have unique benefits that work really well for me.

The Five Minute Journal is an app you can buy for a few bucks that works really well for starting a simple journaling process. Twice a day, once in the morning and once in the evening, you answer a few simple questions: What are you grateful for that day? What have you accomplished? How could you do better? and What you will do to make the day great?

There is also a quote of the day and an option to add a picture for your day from your phone. If you don't use a planner or a journal, start with this. It's cheap, it will remind you to actually use it, and you will see benefits quickly. I also use the reminder option to prompt me to use my other journals, even though they are physical. You can buy the Five Minute Journal in physical format, but I love the app for the reasons stated above and won't be switching.

Another planner I use is called the Freedom Journal. This is a physical journal that will help you accomplish a big goal in one hundred days. In my experience, it's a very effective tool that pushes me to get the right things done on time. There are various review days, but the real benefit is just crafting a plan each morning and reviewing my plan each evening.

I used this journal to write this book. I have a target of writing one thousand words a day, and so far, the Freedom Journal has kept me on track. It's expensive when you compare it to other journals, but it's really well made. And after you hit your big goal, it's fun to look back and see how you did. I only use this planner when I'm in the middle of a big project.

Last, as mentioned above I use the Panda Planner. If you use one planner, use this one. It's a great tool and flexible enough to use for just about anything. There is space for recording monthly, weekly, and daily goals, including exercise, tasks, schedule, priorities, things to be grateful for, and more. Using this every day, along with reviewing monthly and weekly goals every day, is one of the best things you can do for your business.

The SAVERS routine above is built from the Miracle Morning framework. I'm surprised at how much of it seemed ridiculous at first but has ended up being really helpful. If you haven't read one of their books, get *Miracle Morning Millionaires* (much better than *The Miracle Morning for Real Estate Agents* that came out a few years ago).

Real Work

1. After I finish my morning routine, I go through the email on my phone for the first time. I use the Spark email app so that I can easily delete, snooze, or respond. Once I've snoozed or deleted the easy ones, I open my computer and take care of the rest. I don't do anything else until I empty my inbox in the morning.
2. Next, I open Contactually (the customer relationship management software I mentioned earlier) and respond to any prompts. It has me contact between five and fifteen clients a day based on its algorithms and who has responded to me already. It costs about a thousand dollars a year, but it easily brings in thirty times that.
3. Start on daily priorities outlined in Panda Planner.

That's it. By 6:30 a.m., I've usually accomplished everything I have to do that day besides showing property. This opens up my whole day, allowing me to focus on big-picture items, respond quickly to incoming messages, and work on the important things rather than just the urgent things.

I can't overemphasize how waking up early can lead you to more success. If you read about successful people and what their routines are, you'll see that the vast majority do three things almost without fail: they wake up early, they write down their goals, and they practice meditation or prayer regularly. Waking up early may not seem important to you. It wasn't important to me for a long time. But the simple act of getting up a couple hours earlier will change how you do everything else.

For example, I've noticed several important changes just because I started waking up earlier. I watch much less television. When I was staying up later, I tended to watch television at night after the family was in bed. Now I'm asleep by 10 p.m. at the latest and usually have no time for television, other than maybe one show with my wife after the kids go to bed.

My quality time with my family has increased. When I get everything important done before my family even wakes up, I have the flexibility to do more with them. I often take one of my kids out to breakfast or take the day off to go with them to the museum. Getting work done early will feel like a magic trick when you first start doing it consistently. Your weeks will feel like fourteen days instead of seven.

Waking up early will help you be proactive. It's true in every business, but even more so in real estate. The urgent things that come up always trump the important things. If you wait until everyone else is up, you start doing reactive work based on what others need. Then you find it harder and harder to do proactive work. Working proactively over the long haul is the only way to grow your business exponentially. That's the time when you focus on marketing, content creation, planning, goal setting, and much more.

Just waking up earlier will help you implement the habit of building habits and give you more hours to implement your own routine every day. I try to add one new habit a month at least, and having time already set aside in the morning makes this process much easier. Think about habits you would like to build: learning a new language, reading consistently, praying, meditating, daily journaling, planning, goal setting, being grateful, and many, many more. Waking up early makes all these things much easier to accomplish.

By waking up earlier, you will be trading bad for good. At least twice a year, a famous athlete or celebrity gets into trouble at a nightclub at 2 a.m. Invariably, the sports commentator will always follow up the story with, "Nothing good happens after midnight at a nightclub." The same is true for agents.

By waking up earlier, you are starting off the day right. When you start your day proactively, building new habits, thinking of others, reviewing your goals, thinking about where you want to go, clearing your inbox and your CRM, and thinking through your day, you're setting yourself up for a great day. It's nearly impossible to have a bad day at work when you start by knocking so many things out of the park before anyone else is awake.

Waking up early also eliminates the problem of being late. One of my pet peeves is being late for anything or having the person I'm meeting show up late. Waking up early will help eradicate this problem because you're so far ahead that it's hard to mess up your schedule. Being on time for everything you do shows others that you care about them, that you are true to your word, and that you're a professional. Choosing to be late, especially as a habit, shows that you don't care about others, that you can't keep simple promises, and that you are lazy.

Don't buy into the excuse that you are a night person and that it's just not natural for you to wake up early. Commit to not making excuses, and you will at least have clear direction on what is really important to you. Instead of saying, "I would wake up early, but I just can't because I'm a night person," say, "Waking up early and growing my business is not a priority for me because there are other things that are more important."

It's very possible to have other things more important in your life, but if you find yourself staying up to binge-watch *Breaking Bad* or play another hour of *World of Warcraft*, you're not doing anything important. Be brutally honest with yourself. Each of us does exactly what we want to every day. You work the job you have because you either want it or don't want anything else. You want to wind down with a television show rather than wake up earlier.

Work on having a rhythm to your year, your quarter, your week, your day. Building the habit of regularly setting goals, reviewing targets, and tracking your progress will push you forward faster than you think is possible. Remember this quote from Microsoft founder Bill Gates: "Most people overestimate what they can do in one year and underestimate what they can do in ten years." You may not hit all your targets right at first, but keep it up, and you'll be amazed at how much progress you make in just one year if you start setting goals.

Bonus Tip #8:

Focus on listings. There are agents who say that they just like to work with buyers because sellers are too hard to keep happy. In many ways, buyers can be easier to work with and more fun at times. I love the challenge of quickly building rapport with a client in a short amount of time and selling them on using me as their agent while giving them a taste of the area they're interested in.

However, focusing on buyers is a losing strategy, more so now than ever. People look online for property almost exclusively. If you don't have listings online, you won't get calls. When I first started real estate in 2005, our office had six phone lines, and we could expect ten to twelve leads a day. It was a lot of fun to work in the bullpen and feel the energy that comes from juggling multiple calls, emails, and walk-ins. Now we're lucky to get one call a day and one or two walk-ins a week. Nothing has changed other than the advent of clients looking online. We have more listings than ever in our thirty-five years in business and more agents as well. But the listing agents are the ones getting the calls.

Get listings and get them no matter what it takes. My advice to new agents is to pick a smaller neighborhood and start working it regularly. Send every owner a postcard once a month, go knock on doors, offer gifts of cookies for Christmas, and do anything else you can think of. Make yourself the expert for that neighborhood. Once you have a healthy amount of listings, the number of escrowed contracts you have will start to grow by itself.

When you do work with buyers, try to shift your mindset and think of them as future sellers instead of current buyers. You're helping them find a house now, but it's really a listing you'll get five years from now. Once you help someone buy a place, follow up relentlessly and don't give up your advantage to any other agent.

Taking Action

Putting your goals in place and deciding your direction are important steps to make as an agent, but they're just the beginning. If you set goals and then never follow through, you are wasting your time. While the literature on the value of goal setting is vast, little attention is given to actually doing the work to reach those goals.

Humans are unique creatures in many ways, but one of the most fascinating aspects that separate us from animals is how our actions often don't match our intentions. If a dog decides he wants to do something, like run across the yard to pick up a bone, he'll just do it. But when a human decides to do something, it gets much more complicated. We rarely do what we think we want.

The apostle Paul says it this way in Romans 7:15: "For I do not understand my own actions. For I do not do what I want, but I do the very thing I hate." Matching your actions with your intentions is not an easy process, but there are a few tricks that you can use to accomplish your goals.

There is a great book on this subject called *Following Through*.[1] The authors detail seven strategies to help you match action with intention. I've listed a few of those principles below along with my own thoughts on applying them to real estate specifically. Use these to shrink the gap between action and intention, and you'll get more done.

As you read these ideas, remember that we all have this problem. You have no more or less willpower than anyone else. Also remember not to make too many promises. An unkept promise is another nail in the I-can't-do-it coffin. Carefully consider every commitment before you make it. Start small and build on small successes, and you'll be surprised at what you can get done.

Spotlighting

Use cues to remind you to do what's most important. Put reminders of good habits you want to build near or on frequently used items. For example, change the wallpaper of your smartphone to a question like, "Have I made progress on getting a listing today?" Think about the environment where you do most of your real estate work. What can you do to be constantly reminded of the most important action to take every single day?

One of my motivators at work is keeping in mind what I want for my family. Putting a picture of my family next to my office phone helps me remember the real reason I show up every day. I also have our company's core values, purpose statement, and fifty-year vision posted right next to where I sit every day. Having a constant reminder of the direction I want to go at all times keeps me focused.

Think about the things you can do to get the biggest bang for your buck and create cues in your environment to make it happen. If you have a goal to write five handwritten notes each day, leave your stationery on top of your desk instead of tucked away. If you need to update your CRM every morning, set your wallpaper with a reminder to do it first. Spotlighting sounds simple because it is, but it's also a powerful tool to keep your focus in the right place.

Willpower Leveraging

We often run out of willpower in bad situations. For example, it can be hard to make good diet decisions. You may not be able to resist the famous molasses cookies from the local farmer's market once they're in your pantry. Instead, use your willpower to not buy them in the first place. Resisting a purchase at the store is easier than resisting the cookies in your pantry when you are craving a snack at midnight.

Here are some ways you can apply this tool to real estate:

- Use willpower leveraging to avoid distractions. One of the common problems I see with real estate agents is that many waste time as they wait for leads to come in. Eliminate the games on your phone, block Netflix from your computer, and stop the temptation to be distracted before it starts.

- Use willpower leveraging to accomplish big goals. Having a goal to send out five hundred postcards every time you list, sell, or reduce the price on a property requires a lot of willpower to implement all at once. Instead, focus on small goals and build toward easier decisions. For instance, you could easily locate the best profile picture one day, then do a rough draft of the design the next for the just-listed template, and then continue from there.

- Evidence suggests we have a limited amount of willpower to use each day. Be careful how you spend it, or you won't be able to make the really big decisions when the time comes. Make as much of your day an automatic routine as you can. Build habits that don't sap your willpower, and you'll accomplish more over time. Reviewing your goals every day takes a ton of willpower, but if you review goals every day for one quarter, you'll turn your review into a habit. And habits don't require any willpower.

- In *The Willpower Instinct*, Kelly McGonigal argues that the only two ways to actually increase our willpower capacity is through working out and meditation. Building habits is the most effective way to conserve willpower, but consider the additional benefits of working on your mind and body and how this can help you accomplish more.

Creating Compelling Reasons

We often don't follow through with our intentions because the consequences are so far removed from the present. Make the consequences more immediate, and things will get done much faster. Here are some examples of compelling reasons you can use in real estate:

- Commit to sending ten handwritten cards a week. Place ten ten-dollar bills in an envelope. For every card written, move one bill to your wallet. Friday at 5 p.m., if there is any money left, you have to shred it. Making the consequence more immediate is highly motivational. Even though the real consequence of not writing notes or making calls is much greater, having immediate, visceral consequences is surprisingly effective.

- Reward yourself. After a closing, I buy myself a closing gift. It's usually something small, like a book I've had on my wish list for a long time, but I try to reward myself for the good things that happen, reinforcing future behavior.

- Punish yourself. If things aren't going well for you, make the consequences more real. One of the ways I do that is to refuse to eat out if I don't have any contracts in escrow. If I don't have anything going on, I bring a sack lunch to the office and won't go out to eat.

- In *The 4-Hour Chef*, Timothy Ferriss lays out a simple, extremely effective plan for creating powerful consequences for yourself. Just thinking about doing this can be powerful enough to force you to accomplish more so you can avoid having to actually go through with it:
    - Calculate 1–1.5 percent of your annual income.
    - Find a friend to be your accountability partner and to control your funds, someone you trust who is strong enough to carry this through.
    - Choose an anti-charity. What is a cause you just can't stand? Maybe it's the GOP or DNC. Maybe it's PETA. It could

be the presidential library fund for a former president you hated. Pick something you hate. You can use the website www.stickk.com to help choose an anti-charity and post your funds there as well.

⊚ If you don't follow through and accomplish your goal, your friend has to donate the money you pledged to your anti-charity in your name. From then on, your name will be publicly associated with an organization that drives you crazy, and a good chunk of your money will support them.[2]

Baby Steps

Commit only to the absolute easiest part of the task, and then let what happens happen. For example, imagine your goal is to write a book. Instead of focusing on 1,500 words a day, commit to sitting in front of your computer for two minutes every morning with your word processor open. That's so easy that it's hard to fail, and once you're there, you just might start writing.

In real estate, commit to reviewing lists of calls you should make every day, but don't promise to make any. Or commit to putting postcards and envelopes on top of your desk for five minutes but not actually writing any.

This can be a powerful way to start building up small wins that will eventually lead to large changes and great habits. Don't dismiss it because it sounds too simplistic. Give it a try if you struggle staying committed to larger tasks. Being able to accomplish even extremely small tasks each day will turn you into an agent who follows through on what he says, and that's one of the keys to success.

Strike While the Iron Is Hot

Often our good intentions fade over time. If you commit to something, do it right away or at least a small part of it. Otherwise, it may not get done at all. Doing at least a small part of it immediately will take less willpower and is often your best chance of accomplishing it.

If you have a great idea, act on it today instead of waiting until next week. Your chance of actually following through will be much higher if you start while you're excited about it.

Use Your Phone for Good, Not Evil

Our phones can be our greatest asset or our greatest hurdle depending on how we use them. Consider using a reminder app on your phone to build habits and help you accomplish the right things. I use an app called Echo that allows me to set daily, weekly, or even hourly reminders to keep important things at the front of my mind. For instance, every hour from 7 a.m. to 5 p.m., my phone chimes to remind me to clear my inbox and CRM for the day. It's impossible to forget something if you set your phone to remind you of it. Don't allow yourself the excuse of forgetfulness; solve the problem permanently by implementing a system of reminders.

To keep me focused on the important things in life, I also have an app called WeCroak. Five times a day, at random times, it will text me a reminder that I'm going to die one day and then sends an inspirational quotation. Though it may sound morbid, being reminded that life is not permanent is a great way to accomplish what is important in the present and has a long history in philosophical traditions, including Stoicism and Christianity.

Use these principles to follow through on your goals, and you'll be on your way to doing big things. If you want to continue learning about follow-through, here are five books I recommend starting with:

- *Following Through* by Levinson and Greider. This is one of the best books on sticking with your goals and implementing real-word strategies that work.
- *The 4-Hour Chef* by Timothy Ferriss, who also wrote *The 4-Hour Workweek* and *The 4-Hour Body*. There is some great advice in the first section on breaking down goals and making them easily achievable, as well as following through. As a

bonus, you'll learn how to cook the best rib eye you can make from home.

- *Eat That Frog!* by Brian Tracy. This is the best of Brian Tracy's books. It's short and offers extremely practical advice on striking while the iron is hot.

- *Decisive* by Chip Heath and Dan Heath. This is a fascinating look at how we make decisions—the best book I've read on making decisions and setting goals you can actually follow through on. One of my favorite techniques they teach is the 10-10-10 rule. Ask yourself how you will feel about a decision in ten minutes, ten months, and ten years.

- *Miracle Morning Millionaires* by Hal Elrod and David Osborne is by far the best of the Miracle Morning book series. It shows that one of the best ways to make sure you accomplish your goals is to wake up earlier and get started on goals before anything else. This book will help you do that.

Bonus Tip #9:

How do you know what people think about your business? Don't assume your branding and marketing are getting through in the right way. One very practical way to find out what people think about you is to ask a dozen people who have some familiarity with you a simple question: "What is the first word you think of when you think of my business?"

The answers will yield surprising results, and you may find that you have some natural advantages you've been neglecting. If 60 percent of your market thinks of you as having integrity as your highest priority, but your marketing focuses on a technological advantage, you're not marketing to your strengths. When your target market already thinks of you in a certain way, find ways to enhance and capitalize on it rather than fight it.

Once you know what others think of your business, you can work on nailing down your USP (unique selling proposition). This

---

is the one thing that makes you stand out in your market from any other option, stated shortly and succinctly. In my market, my USP is "I wrote the book on buying and selling Texas farm and ranch property." Everything else I do promotes that idea and goes back to it.

Don't waste any space, and never waste your money on brand-building. Leave the brand-building for the national brokerages to worry about. As an agent, you need to know if your marketing is working, and you need to know it quickly so you can adjust as needed.

Many agents send out market updates on postcards but don't have any instructions on how to respond. Even something as simple as "Call for a free market evaluation" is missing from many advertisements. Think about something unique that you can offer and ask them to call you to get it. On my advertising, I often promote my book as a free resource. All they have to do is call and request it. When I get that call, they are opening the door for me to send them a lot more than just one book. I put together a package and send them the following:

- *Personalized postcard handwritten by me*
- *Copy of my book*
- *Multiple business cards*
- *Interview sheet with the top ten questions to ask your farm and ranch agent*
- *Free report on saving money on taxes for land owners*
- *Free report on improving your land for resale value quickly*
- *History of our company*
- *Coupon for a local restaurant*
- *And more . . .*

Marketing doesn't have to be complicated, but as Dan Kennedy says, you want it to be magnetic. The goal in marketing is not to continually push everything you are doing, but to whet people's appetites for what you have already done so that they request your services. If someone asks you for information and material, then you already have a huge head start on the competition.

Real Estate Psychology 101

"The greatest discovery of any generation is that
a human can alter his life by altering his attitude."

—William James

Real Estate and Influence

Real estate is a great business to experiment with different sales approaches and techniques. What has worked really well for me may not work in the same way for you. Your own personality, target market, brokerage, and countless other factors will inform the methods that work best for you. But there are timeless principles and systems that will pay off over and over again if you put in the time. They are much harder to learn than a simple trick or tactic, but putting the time in to learn principles will pay huge dividends for you.

There are many areas you could study, but perhaps none of them is more important than psychology. Since humans are complicated creatures, it's extremely difficult to see why we make the decisions we make. Studying timeless psychological principles will give you an edge few other real estate agents have. For example, it may be easy to print off a template letter from a real estate marketing company and just use that for your marketing. However, if you don't understand the underlying psychology behind the letter, you aren't making lasting progress.

Learning how and why these principles of psychology work will earn you more commissions and influence than you thought was possible. Before we start, here are a few words of caution.

People are influenced in very odd, irrational ways. There are ways to twist people's arms, manipulating them for your own benefit.

Don't fall into the trap of using these principles for anything like that. It will work in the short term, but breaking ethical boundaries and focusing on short-term gains is a losing strategy. Instead, use these principles for your clients' best interests. Use them to get your clients the best deal, to help them see why you are truly the best real estate agent for their needs, to get past the objections stopping them from making a good decision. The two prerequisites you should have firmly in place before using these principles are these:

1. Commit to your clients' best interests and resolve not to cross any moral or ethical boundaries.
2. Be an expert in your field. This is easier than it sounds in real estate, because most agents don't know what they're doing. Most agents are part-time and just using real estate to supplement a retirement income. Commit to knowing more than 95 percent of your competition, and you will be an expert.

Weapons of Influence

When you become a real estate agent, you should also become a dedicated learner and reader. Of all the psychology books and books on business I have read, *Influence* by Robert Cialdini is the most valuable and the one I return to the most. The following six weapons of influence are detailed in this classic book. I'll explain the underlying principle and give a few examples that apply specifically to real estate for each, but I cannot recommend highly enough that you buy this book and study it yourself.

Cialdini defines weapons of influence as "fixed-action patterns" that can be both exploited and protected against.[1] We are all creatures of habit and are influenced by unseen principles, whether we want to admit it or not. As we become more and more sophisticated, the power these weapons of influence can hold actually increases. The busier we are as a society and as individuals, the more we're forced to rely on automatic behavior patterns to get through our day. These behavior patterns can be engaged by savvy marketers (and real estate agents) who need to get their point across in a world that gets noisier all the time.

Reciprocity

The power of reciprocity is one of the most powerful tools you can use as a real estate agent, and it's often very easy to implement. The reciprocity rule is simply an ingrained behavior pattern that makes us want to repay others for a good deed done to us. If someone does a favor for us, we feel indebted to them until we right the scales, so to speak.

The reciprocity rule is an overwhelming force that triggers subconscious behaviors. Think about how marketers and companies use this rule to engage your own behavior patterns. For example, many stores offer free samples to shoppers as they walk around. They are giving away their merchandise for free to engage the reciprocity rule in the buyers who accept the sample. No matter how small the sample, most buyers will feel a sense of indebtedness until they can resolve it.

This is one reason why you should never accept a so-called *free* gift unless you are prepared to accept what comes after it. Whether it's a religious group going door to door in your neighborhood or someone providing free marketing help online, recognize the reciprocity rule for what it is. There is no such thing as a free lunch. This is also why you should avoid saying yes to free drinks at a bar when someone offers them to you, unless you are prepared to feel indebted to that person.

One of the reasons the reciprocity rule works so well is that it's hard to refuse a gift. We are wired to give, but we have an even stronger desire to accept what is offered. Then, a favor must be met with a favor. Note what that means for you as an agent. **Accepting a favor or a gift can be an even stronger influencer than giving one.** If a client offers you something, say yes. I love going to listing appointments where I'm in someone's house. When I'm offered a drink and say yes, I've started the process of building rapport through reciprocity. Here are some practical ways to use the reciprocity rule in real estate:

- When you go on an appointment, bring a cooler full of water, sparkling water, and other beverages to offer to your client.
- Prepare an introduction-to-the-community gift for your buyers when you first meet with them.
- When a client offers you something, accept it: water, gum, or even advice. The reciprocity rule can be engaged with a psychological exchange or a physical exchange.
- When you give something to a client, back it up with gift language when it's appropriate. For example, when I give away my book, I often say, "Please accept this gift. It may be helpful for you as you look around for property."
- Buy your client closing gifts. For some reason, this seems to have fallen out of favor, but it's a powerful tool. Make the last interaction with a client a positive one, and they'll overlook some of the difficulties they may have experienced during the contract phase.
- Buy your clients lunch or coffee if possible while you are out showing. This will reinforce that you are giving both your time and money to help them find the right property.
- Use gifts to retain clients. I give my clients cookies or a pie every Thanksgiving to thank them for working with me, even if it's been years since they bought property. This simple gesture helps ensure I'm top of mind when they decide to list and that I don't give up the initial advantage.
- In the same way, I also send physical, handwritten notes to clients after I meet with them to thank them for their time.
- Few agents give gifts, period. You can use this to your advantage, depending on how aggressively you want to gain clients.

I have mailed welcome gifts to people moving to my area even when they weren't my clients and earned their business.

- When I go on a listing appointment, I never present a price the first time I'm there, if I can help it. One reason I like to do this is that the second visit is a great opportunity to give your prospective client a gift. I've won multimillion-dollar listings by bringing a pie on my second visit to thank a client for interviewing me.

Again, these weapons of influence are activating behavior patterns that are already there. When you give gifts to your clients, make sure you're also giving them better service than any other real estate agent possibly could and that you're focused on their long-term goals, not yours. Another great reason to use influence, especially for listings, is that your clients will recognize you're going the extra mile to build rapport with them. If you'll go the extra mile to win them as clients, they know you'll also go the extra mile to sell their house, negotiate the best contract for them, and build up good working relationships with other agents.

Commitment and Consistency

Humans are influenced by personal consistency. For example, if we have acted in a certain way or supported a particular decision, we are much more likely to continue to do so.

There are two main reasons for this consistency bias. The first is that it's a useful shortcut. If we had to re-evaluate every decision each time we received new information, nothing would get done. It's much easier to continue down the path we've already started. The other reason we will stay consistent is that we don't want to know the truth. We would rather be consistently wrong than change our minds and be right.

The key to activating this principle is the initial commitment. Any small step in one direction makes it much more likely for you to keep moving in that direction. The commitment-and-consistency rule is a powerful tool in real estate, both when dealing with others and when influencing yourself. Here are some practical ways I use this principle in my own business:

- Write down your goals. It's not enough to just have goals. You must write them down to fully activate this principle in your own life. Writing down your goals trains your brain and your actions to align with the goals you have on paper. It's a powerful way to influence yourself and get more accomplished. Do not ignore it.
- When you sell a property, the client is committed to using you as a real estate agent. You should always keep this commitment at the top of both your and his mind and not let it go. The old cliché "Your best client is the one you already have" is especially true in real estate.
- When a client is struggling to decide on a property, one of the best ways you can overcome their mental block is by filling out a draft of a contract. Drafting lowers the pressure of actually presenting an offer, and walking the client through the process helps him feel more confident about his decision.
- I always fill out a listing agreement and take it with me on listing appointments. As we talk about the details of the contract, I'll pull it out and fill in the few blanks we talk through together—typically the listing price, listing term, and any variable commission rates. By moving the conversation from verbal to written, you activate the commitment principle.
- Having the listing agreement with you and filling it out is a great way to push one step further. If the timing is right, you can ask if the clients are ready to go ahead and list. If they say no or that they would still like to think about it, you haven't lost anything. Just explain you're going to leave the listing there for review.

- A classic real estate sales technique consists of clarifying any objections the client has to a particular property. For example, if one property was close but not quite right, nail down exactly what it was that was missing. Let's say it didn't have a downstairs master bedroom, and the clients prefer to be on the west side of town. You can then use the consistency principle by asking them to affirm something like the following: "So, what you're saying is that if I can find you a similar property on the west side of town that has a downstairs master, then you would be ready to write an offer on it?"

- Remind clients of the relationships and commitments you share. This reminder could include past real estate transactions but could also cover many other areas. I often help people in my church buy and sell their properties. Clients and agents are more comfortable when they have strong, shared commitments outside of real estate. Shared commitments cause sellers to list with their friends more often than not. The commitment principle trumps any other advantage when it comes to landing the interview.

- One word of warning with this principle: don't use the lowball technique that car dealers have made famous. Once you commit to buying a car for a ridiculously low price, then the salesman starts ratcheting the price up for new reasons: his manager won't let him sell that low, he overlooked some features on the car, and other excuses. Don't try this in real estate. It's shady, and many people are on guard for deceptive techniques when they are talking with an agent.

The commitment-and-consistency technique is a powerful tool for selling real estate, but its best use is in influencing yourself. Use this influence principle to become a better real estate agent by writing down your goals and aiming high for what you want to achieve. The results will often feel like magic, but it's nothing more than forcing your actions to align with what you have already committed to via the consistency principle.

By contrast, if you aren't ready to commit to success in real estate by writing your goals down on paper, then your daily habits and actions will not last. Without a commitment to align to, you will gravitate toward whatever is easiest in the moment.

Social Proof

In an uncertain situation, there is little time to evaluate everything we need to know. In these circumstances, social proof is one of the main tools we use to quickly evaluate whether someone is trustworthy, desirable, or likable. We all rely on how others interact to form our own opinions.

That's the way social proof works, and we are all guilty of it. The world would be impossible to navigate if we couldn't evaluate quickly based on others' actions and make decisions for ourselves. For example, ratings systems that rank popular media strongly influence what we watch, read, or listen to. I love podcasts, and I will often scroll through the highest-ranked podcasts in different categories before deciding what to download. After all, if that many people have already listened to it, then it must be good.

There are many examples in other spheres as well. Some churches put money in the offering plate before it's passed around to increase the number of people who give. The same is true for your local coffee shop's tip jar. Ever notice how there are already a few bills in the jar even if you're the first one there? They have learned the principle of social proof: others have already tipped, so you should too.

When a given situation is uncertain, we are much more likely to use social proof to make decisions. Real estate is often a very uncertain situation, whether you are working on getting a listing or securing a commitment from a buyer, and social proof is one of the best tools you can use to your advantage. Without using social proof, you could lose clients who just don't have the time to evaluate and make the correct decision. Here are some ways you can use social proof in real estate:

- Referrals. Real estate agents have always known that referrals are the best source of business. Referrals function on the principle of social proof. Ask your clients for referrals and figure out ways to reward them. I often send a gift card as a thank you when I get a referral.
- Reviews. If you don't have referrals to rely on, use testimonials or reviews liberally. When I interview for a listing, I often bring a list of recent testimonials from other clients. This works best when you can connect the dots and show how these clients are similar to your new prospect.
- Google reviews and Zillow rating. More and more clients are using online tools to vet whom they hire. If you don't pay attention to your reviews online, especially on important websites, you will lose out.
- Stories. Often when I drive clients around for the first time, I tell stories about recent transactions with satisfied customers. This is a great way to show your clients that you've helped others just like them, that you have done it successfully, and that you can navigate any issues that come up.
- Organizations. Connect yourself publicly to organizations that vet others. These could include real estate organizations, churches, nonprofits, chambers of commerce, and others.
- Attire. Pay attention to what you wear. Before showing property to new clients for the first time, I often Google them to find out any information I can. If there is something obvious I can connect to, I bring it up while we're out. For example, if I see that they graduated from Texas A&M, where I studied,

I will most likely wear an A&M shirt while showing. If I see they graduated from Texas Tech, I look for other points of connection (like the fact that my dad went there and that I was born in Lubbock, where Texas Tech is located).

- Relationships. Develop great local relationships. I love using this technique because it's a natural, easy way to show new people how much you invest in the community. I frequently take new clients to one of the local restaurants I like. Invariably, the owner will talk to us, tell my clients I'm the best real estate agent he knows, thank them for coming in, and tell them how much they'll like it in the area.

Social proof is one of the most powerful tools you have as an agent. You should never feel guilty for highlighting organizations you've been a part of, asking for referrals, or showing other prospects your testimonials from past clients. People have a limited amount of time to make decisions, and by giving your prospective clients social proof, you give them the tools they need to make an informed decision. Use social proof as a shortcut to show exactly who you are and highlight your best qualities quickly, because you often won't have the time with clients to get to know them any other way.

Liking

The next principle of influence is liking, which should surprise no one. We do business with people more often when we like them. We tend to say yes to people we like a lot more often than we say yes to those we don't like. Liking is the reason you will lose listings to an agent who only sells three properties a year, because that agent has invested twenty years of relationship building and liking with that particular client.

This principle should be used liberally but also ethically. Never fake something to build rapport faster. This kind of manipulation is disgusting, unethical, and unnecessary. We all have ways to identify with clients honestly, without resorting to cheap tricks. If you get caught in a lie, you'll get burned. I don't fish, so I would never pretend I did to connect with a prospect. As soon as he asked what kind of lure I preferred, disaster would strike. Here are some other ways to use liking to your advantage:

- Physical attractiveness. Don't be embarrassed to highlight your best physical features. Research shows that being physically attractive will cause others to assume you are also talented, kind, honest, smart, and many other positive traits. There is a halo effect from physical attractiveness that changes how others view you.

- Boost attractiveness. If you aren't naturally a supermodel, don't worry. Physical attractiveness is genetic, but there are many things you can do to improve how you are perceived. This includes frequent haircuts, working out regularly, losing weight, gaining muscle, wearing sharper clothes and shoes, eating healthy, whitening your teeth, getting a new car, and many other factors.

  Attractive people in our society enjoy an enormous advantage. Work on maximizing what you can use, and you will increase your sales and likability.

- Similarities. Look for ways that you are honestly like the other person and highlight those instances. Similarity is just one of the factors that falls under the principle of liking, but it is worth special attention because it is misused so often.

  Finding points of honest similarity is a great way to increase your likability quickly and build rapport without risk. You will have your own similar traits to highlight with your clients and prospects, but here are some I use frequently:

- School. Many of my clients went to the same college I did because it is near the area I work. I always wear my college ring, and it's helped me sell many properties.
- Kids. I have four kids, an easy connection point with both parents and grandparents.
- Food. I love great food. I love talking about our local food and what's good in our area.
- Vehicles. If I happen to drive the same brand of car, I mention it.
- Reading. I love to read and often have a few books in my truck when I show. If the client likes reading too, it's an easy conversation to build on.
- Homeschooling. We homeschool our kids, giving me great things to talk about if someone is interested in alternative education.
- Showing property. I have found many of my clients wish they were an agent, especially an agent showing country property. Sometimes you can build on the similarity principle when someone wants to know more about your job. I often encourage my clients to get their real estate license, and a few have taken me up on it.
- Investments. I invest in property, land, and homes, so I can relate to my clients in that way. I will often share the details of properties I have bought and sold that are similar to the kind of property they are interested in.
- Home. When my clients focus on a home similar to mine, I drive them by my house and the last two places I lived in. This technique is a great way to show I'm interested in the same kind of home they are.
- Sports. It is always easy to talk about local sports teams and what's going on with the professional teams located near you.

- ◉ Weather. Classic small talk for good reason. The weather is immediately shared with those you talk to about it and it is valuable information to have.
- Compliments. When you compliment people, they will be much more likely to think favorably of you. Amazingly, this is true even if they know the compliment is fake. Fortunately, there is no reason to not be completely genuine. Look for opportunities to compliment your clients honestly—on their car, business, recent retirement, taste in homes, children, or a variety of other natural things that come up.
- Think about the people you like the most in your own life. You probably see them much more frequently than you see those you don't like. We spend time with those we like and seek multiple interactions with them. Here are some ways you can use this as a real estate agent:
  - ◉ I always try to double my appointments when I interview for a listing. I go once to meet them and take a tour, then wait a few days to go back with my analysis. Getting in front of a client twice when most agents only show up once is a large advantage.
  - ◉ In the same way, look for opportunities to increase your meetings with your clients. Never miss an opportunity to meet up with them, even if they just want to drive by a property or check something out from the road. Meet them every chance you get.
  - ◉ Even seeing a client twice in one day can increase likability. If you can't go with your clients to lunch, send them off by themselves and then reconnect after. This break allows you to see them twice in one day.
- Associate yourself with good news. Meteorologists are blamed for bad weather and praised for good weather. Remember that what you're associated with will reflect on you, so highlight

your associations. For example, talk about your favorite sports team after a big win. Wear the team colors if you can.

- Associate yourself with food. One of the best places to meet a new prospect or client is over a meal or a cup of coffee. Studies have shown that you should drink something hot because your clients will feel warmer toward you. If you meet over a meal, make sure it's great. Ideally it should be a unique enough meal to stand out as special.

There are so many opportunities to connect with a prospect that you should never have to resort to dishonesty. If you really struggle to honestly connect with someone—this definitely happens to me sometimes—don't fight it. Instead, refer the person to another agent in your office you know will connect better. You will still get paid and, more importantly, the client will be taken care of. Focus your time on prospects you connect with easily and on multiple levels, and you will build a business that lasts a lifetime.

Authority

When you get pulled over by a police officer, you are primed to listen and be influenced. We are wired to listen to those with authority and pay more attention to what they say. Developing and conveying authority is one of the best ways an agent can gain the respect and ears of clients.

If you've sold real estate for any length of time, you've run into clients who assume you have zero authority, that you just completed some online courses and received a piece of paper that allows you to sell real estate, that you have no special knowledge about the business. This attitude can quickly turn into a problem. When others assume you don't know what you're talking about, you lose all authority.

As a real estate agent who focuses on clients' needs, you have a responsibility to convey your authority and establish it quickly. If you aren't working on building your authority, you are costing both yourself and your clients money. Here are some ways you can build authority as a real estate agent:

- Publishing. Writing a book was hard, but it's the best thing I've done for my business. Just by having a published book, I can establish my authority in minutes and become the expert without any other need for proving it. I have also allowed the agents in my firm to use the book and present it as a product of the brokerage.

- Titles. As an agent, there are many other titles you can gain to convey authority. As you decide which to pursue, remember that your clients have no idea what it means when you have a lot of acronyms behind your name. The most important designation you can gain, by far, is that of broker. Even if the general public doesn't quite understand what a broker is, my experience is that clients respect a broker a lot more than an agent.

- Size. One of my natural advantages as a real estate agent is that I'm almost six-and-a-half-feet tall. Size and status are related in our minds, so use your height to help raise your authority if you have it. I wear boots every day, which make me even taller. No matter what size you are, consider wearing boots or high heels, and you'll inspire greater authority. (Hint: I always try to present any lowball offers in person to other agents because of my height. I've found even a lowball offer is taken more seriously when I can hand it directly to the agent.)

- Dress. Your daily dress should be carefully considered and promote authority. Depending on where you're working and who your clients are, your dress will change drastically. I started my career trying to get by with wearing flip-flops to show country property, and that quickly exposed how little expertise I had.

- Be an expert. Perhaps the hardest hurdle to overcome as an agent is establishing expertise. If you want authority, you should not just use the shortcuts of nice clothes and taller boots. Take extra classes, shadow your broker, read more books like this, and commit to getting your broker's license as soon as you can.

- Create small reports. I understand that a book can be an overwhelming project, but consider writing reports that convey your authority as well. I've penned small reports on the tax advantages of selling your primary home, investment strategies for raw land, the seven most important things you need to know before buying, and many other topics.

- Shape the conversation. Imagine this: you walk into an interview for a listing, and the seller asks a dozen tough questions about you, your company, how you market, and how you're different from any other agent. You are completely prepared and answer each question immediately, proving your expertise, market knowledge, and professionalism. If you could do that with every listing appointment and know for sure that your competition wouldn't be half as prepared as you are, you could win a lot more listings. Here's how to make this happen every time you go on a listing appointment: give the seller a one-page sheet of questions to ask his agent before listing. It's that simple. Remember that people rarely buy and sell homes (or other properties) and often don't know the right questions to ask. Every time I use this technique, my prospective clients ask me questions directly off the page I have given them. Of course, I'm always prepared to answer because I'm the one who provided the questions. This is one of the most powerful listing tools I use.

- Don't be afraid to say, "I don't know." Being an authority on a subject doesn't mean you know everything there is to know about it. When a client asks you a question you're unsure of, don't give a slick answer that may or may not be true. A real authority on a subject knows there is always more to learn and

88

will prove his or her value by getting the best answer from the best source quickly. Not answering a question right away allows you to follow up with your client rather than just calling to see if he's ready to make an offer. Be a real authority and prove you can get the answers they need quickly.

- Use others' authority when needed. Get to know the agents in your office so you can draw on their expertise when you need it. At every appointment, I provide a document that highlights many of the unique qualities and skills of agents in our office. Even though I'm not a ranch manager, a wildlife expert, or a home stager, I show that I have access to those folks and that we work together.

- Likewise, don't be afraid to give up part of your commission by bringing in another agent if his or her skill set will land the deal. Before you get a listing or have a committed buyer, there is a fierce competition for your prospect's attention. If you sense that bringing in another agent as a partner would put you over the top, jump on the opportunity. You will have the favor returned in the future, and commission sales is an all-or-nothing game—you don't get anything for almost getting a listing.

Authority is one of the harder things to prove as a new agent, but now you have some good ideas for building your authority quickly and piggybacking on others when you have to. The ability to influence through authority is powerful, and having real credentials to rely on will help your business take off.

Scarcity

This is the last of the six psychological principles that Cialdini focuses on, and it also happens to be the most overused in real estate. False scarcity is used so often by agents that it's lost much of its power. How many times have you heard, "Well, we have a lot of interest in that one; there may be an offer coming in. Be sure your buyer moves fast."

The principle of scarcity is simple. Opportunities will seem more valuable to us when their availability is limited. If something is limited by either time or quantity, then we will want it more and be willing to pay more for it. Fear of missing out (FOMO) is so deeply ingrained in us that we have an everyday acronym for it. If something is about to disappear, or if a lot of other people want it at the same time, it automatically becomes more valuable to us.

Here are a few ways you can effectively use the scarcity principle as a real estate agent:

1. Be honest. Always tell other agents and clients the truth about other activity and whether there are other offers coming in. I've made this a practice from the beginning; therefore, when I have genuine activity and other offers to report, the report carries much more weight with me than it does with some other agents.

   Unfortunately, it may take a while to earn some clients' trust. I recently had a client who lost out on a three-million-dollar deal they really wanted, but they couldn't quite come to terms with the seller's counter. I communicated the other interest in the property honestly and told them I thought it would sell, but they were wary from dealing with other agents and chose to wait it out.

   The downside is that they lost out on a deal they wanted. The upside is that they now know I'm honest with them. When the next property comes along, there's a much better chance we'll jump on it at the right time and get a deal done.

2. Make yourself scarce. Too many real estate agents jump at every chance to work with a client regardless of their schedule. When someone calls and asks if you can show a property sometime next week, you should rarely answer, "Absolutely, any day works. I'm wide-open." That shows you aren't in demand. If you're too

available, others automatically assume you must not be great at your job, or more people would be working with you.

Instead, if someone asks to see property with you next week, use the either/or principle. Say something like, "I have Wednesday morning or Friday around 2 p.m. open. Do either of those times work for you?" You aren't letting them know you really have the entire week open, but you're giving them options.

What happens if they say neither of those times work? Ask them, "What day and time would be best for your schedule?" Once they let you know, tell them you can move some things around so that will work. Can you call them back in ten minutes and confirm? Taking the time to not be completely available shows you're in demand, and your clients will listen to you more once they realize this.

Even if you have to fake it 'til you make it, your schedule will soon fill up, and scarcity will be a necessity if you're building your business the right way. I show property on any day or night at any time, but I also make sure the showings work with my schedule and the other things I have planned.

3. You can use scarcity even if there are no other properties in play. My market is largely a second-home/retirement-home market—in other words, a luxury real estate market. Buyers usually don't have to buy anytime soon, and sellers are almost never desperate to sell. That means that properties sit on the market longer, the buyers search longer, and the relationships take more time to build.

Knowing your market well and explaining this to your buyers and sellers can make a big difference. The reality for sellers in this kind of market is that buyers are scarce for most properties. There aren't many who can afford and desire exactly what the sellers already have, so if someone shows interest, we should take that interest seriously. It may be months before a better buyer comes along, and it can cost a lot of money to wait.

At the same time, a seller who has time to wait can bank on the unique features of the property even if it is priced above market. It's often extremely difficult to price property in a luxury market because there are so few comparable properties that really fit. I often explain to my buyers exactly what the comparable market says, but also point to my experience if my gut tells me it will sell at a higher price anyway.

Pricing correctly can drive scarcity. This is especially true when you have a large buyer pool in a particular segment. Sellers often want to overprice and see what happens, but if you price correctly in a busy market, you may get a premium. Recently, I listed a house in town for 20 percent more than it was purchased for a year ago. I explained that this price was a premium, but we could get lucky. In one day, we had two full-price offers. One was cash, but I was able to get them to pay extra for appliances. We also leveraged the other offer waiting in the wings to prevent the buyers from asking for any repairs. Because we priced right, we took advantage of the scarcity principle at every stage of the contract, and my sellers were able to make a tidy profit on their home.

4. Future scarcity can drive current sales. Be sure you point out future scarcity to your clients if it exists. Two examples in our market are antique homes, which no one is building anymore, and raw land with a great building site. In both cases, these properties are priced at a premium now but should only increase in the future. As more new homes are built, the percentage of antique homes in our market will shrink at the same time their value is going up.

As builders continue developing raw land, there will be fewer building sites for dream homes. It's already very rare to find an ideal homesite on small acreage in our market and, in the future, these sites will continue to get a rich premium.

5. I have not tried this next tactic, but I have thought about it. I may experiment with it in the future, but for now I'll share it as an idea here in case it helps you brainstorm other ideas. Would you be willing to create scarcity by strictly limiting the number of listings you take? If you only have a dozen listings at a time, you could use that to leverage your way into higher-priced listings. This is a risky strategy because I hate to turn down listings, but it could be a unique advantage if your market is right for it.

Scarcity is a powerful principle of influence, but one you should use cautiously as a real estate agent. Remember that until you prove your character, many of your clients will assume you're lying, simply using the scarcity principle to push a faster, higher offer. Be patient and use scarcity honestly to build up trust with your client. Then, when there is true scarcity, you can honestly convey the message to your client and get the contract escrowed.

Influence Principles in Real Estate

Before you engage in a real estate activity, think through these principles and come up with unique ways to apply them in different circumstances. I've included a few examples in the following pages, but there are hundreds of different ways you can apply these principles in ways unique to your own personality, community, and particular business.

Influence Principles Applied to a Listing Appointment

- Reciprocity: After the listing appointment, send the client a dozen cookies from a local restaurant with a handwritten card as a thank-you gift for the interview. If offered anything from the seller, accept it (drink, snack, etc.).
- Commitment: Bring the listing agreement to the appointment, start talking through the different options that are negotiable, and have your clients make decisions about what they want the agreement to say.

- Social Proof: Bring up your website and show video testimonials during the listing appointment. Show them how many properties you sold last year, highlighting any properties similar to their own.
- Liking: Focus on putting your best foot forward from the first moment you meet. Dress neatly, offer a firm handshake, smile the entire time, and use a lot of eye contact. Find reasons to share laughter with your client during the appointment and point out similarities.
- Authority: Show your expertise by critiquing things that need to be changed on the property in order for clients to realize your full value. Provide an interview sheet they can use to interview you and others on important questions.
- Scarcity: When setting up the appointment, don't be too available with your time. Be sure to mention the other listings you currently have that are similar.

Influence Principles Applied to Meeting a New Buyer Prospect
- Reciprocity: Anytime you're showing, have something small to give the buyers. Bring bottles of water for drinking, coloring books and crayons for kids, and anything else to make them comfortable. Look for an opportunity to buy them coffee or even lunch.
- Commitment: At first contact with a prospect in Texas, you must have your prospects sign a form acknowledging they've received information about brokerage service. This simple acknowledgment is a great way to enact the commitment principle with new prospects.
- Social Proof: While showing properties, point out other places you have sold. Also, provide recent testimonials in their buyer packet along with property information. Establish your credibility by showing that others have worked with you.

Real Estate and Influence

- Liking: Find similarities and point them out quickly. Find out what the clients are looking for in their move and relate it to some of the things you've found by living in the same area.
- Authority: I love showing new prospects in my area of expertise for the first time because I can show my knowledge of the area. Don't just show a few properties—act as a tour guide for the area and point out the best restaurants, events, and other things to do.
- Scarcity: Try to show only three to five homes by ruling out ones that aren't a fit before you see them. Be honest about whether it's a buyer's market or a seller's market, and tell stories about any recent quick sales you've had.

How to Change Someone's Mind

Changing someone's mind is one of the hardest feats in any profession, much less real estate. The technique below uses a person's own reasons and encourages him to persuade himself to change his mind. This technique is detailed in the book *Instant Influence: How to Get Anyone to Do Anything—FAST* by Michael Pantalon, but here is the basic framework you can start using today:

1. How ready are you to change on a scale of one to ten, one meaning "not ready at all" and ten meaning "totally ready"?
2. Why didn't you pick a lower number? (If one was chosen, ask question one again but modify it: "What would it take to turn that one into a two?")
3. What's the next step, if any?[2]

The power of this formula lies in question two, "Why didn't you pick a lower number?" This is contrary to the way most of us think about changing someone else's mind, or even our own minds. Rather than concentrating on why it's not higher, which forces you to look at the negative aspects of the decision, this question forces you to look at all the positive reasons for it being this high.

In real estate, the inventory is always limited. There will be times when your client needs to talk through her options and find her own reasons for moving forward on a particular property or not. This technique can be a powerful tool to help your clients carefully consider their decision. Here's an example of how it can play out, modified for real estate:

> Agent: "On a scale of one to ten, how much do you like this property, one being 'not at all' and ten being 'we love it and are ready to make an offer'?"
> Client: "I would put it at a seven right now."
> Agent: "That's interesting. Why did you choose a seven instead of a six?"
> Client: "Well, there are a lot of good things about this home. We love the wood floors, the updated kitchen, and the natural light in the dining room. We could see ourselves living here."
> Agent: "All good points. Sounds like there is a lot to like in this one."

That's it. By going through this exercise, you encourage your clients to reaffirm the positive aspects of the property and to verbalize their own reasons for making a decision.

This is a great tool to have in your toolbox, not only for real estate but for life in general. Helping others reinforce their own reasoning is a great way to influence others.

Bonus Tip #10

I have talked with a lot of new agents who ask my advice on building rapport with clients faster. How do you connect with clients on a deeper level, faster?

Surprisingly, many new agents have not purchased their own home yet. My first suggestion is to do this if you haven't, no matter what. Go through the process and buy something, even if it's not your dream home. You won't understand the anxiety that comes from making the biggest purchase of your life until you go through the process yourself.

As an investor, I have purchased dozens of properties at this stage in my career. It still gives me an adrenaline rush every time, and it helps me keep in mind what first-time home buyers and other clients go through when they buy a property. Remember that stress level when you're dealing with a client who's acting crazy and give them some grace.

The Psychology of Negotiation

When you're negotiating a real estate deal, there is no greater skill than saying no in a nice way. When you receive an offer or a counteroffer and can say no gracefully, you can force the other side to negotiate against themselves and come back to you with an even better price. There are few things more gratifying than saving your client significant money by forcing the other party to reevaluate their position.

Here are some of my favorite ways to say no:

Silence. Often when you receive an undesirable offer, remaining silent can convey your no to the other party. If the offer is really low, a sigh or a sharp intake of breath before the silence can work wonders. Remember that most people hate negotiating, including real estate agents, and by just being quiet you are forcing the tension to build up.

Usually, another agent will clarify the offer and give you valuable information, such as "This is not a final offer" or "We really want to end up halfway between where we are and where your client is now."

Fair. In *Never Split the Difference*, author Chris Voss spends a lot of time talking about the power of this word. If silence doesn't work, you can use the word *fair* to help reinforce your own position and to say no nicely. We are all wired to be fair to others. If someone accuses us of being unfair, we immediately look at our actions more closely. If you receive a low offer for your client, you can use this principle to your advantage by saying, "My clients really wanted something closer to list price. They just want what's fair. Do you understand what I am saying?"

Mirroring. Mirroring is basically imitation, and it's something you already do unconsciously. Anytime you're with a friend and find your steps in sync or cross your arms in a similar way, you are mirroring. The principle behind mirroring is that we are attracted to similarity but find it harder to connect when others are not in sync with us.

By using the mirroring principle with intention, you can build rapport more quickly with prospects, clients, other agents, and anyone else you come across. Mirroring can be used in person, over the phone, and even through email to help build relationships quickly. Remember that we all use mirroring subconsciously, and much of what this chapter will point out is how to be more aware of what we're already doing and to direct our behavior more effectively.

Perhaps the easiest use of mirroring is simply mirroring words. You can mirror any mode of communication, allowing people to open up and explain further. Very simply, repeat the last three words your client says as a question. Here's an example:

> Client: "We really want to move because we love the community in Hartsville."
> Agent: "Community in Hartsville?"

Practice this technique today in at least three different conversations and see if it works. By mirroring, you're showing your clients that you are invested, that you want them to elaborate, and that you are in sync with what they're thinking. You will see a big difference.

Another way we naturally mirror one another is by matching the tempo and tone of voice of our conversation partner. The next time you meet someone for the first time, pay attention to whether he's speaking faster or slower than you are and if his volume is louder or softer than yours. Changing both your tempo and your volume to be more in sync will establish rapport.

Mirroring body language can be very effective but should happen organically. If someone crosses her arms and then you immediately imitate her, the effect could backfire and cause you to lose rapport. I pay attention to body language to gauge rapport in a conversation. If I notice we are mirroring body language, then I know we're building rapport quickly. On the other hand, if I notice there is a disconnect, I try to figure out what's missing and improve our rapport.

Again, for real estate agents, I caution against mirroring body language consciously because a client might interpret this as insincere. If you decide to try it, don't mirror physical actions immediately. Instead, wait two or three minutes and then mirror an action. Putting some space between the initial action and the mirror will help you have more success with this strategy.

One of my favorite ways to mirror is through email communication. As agents, many of our first interactions with someone new will come via email. In an email you can mirror many different things, including the greeting, sentence length, structure, and salutation.

Did the person use *dear* before your name in the email? Did he use your name at all or just go straight to the body of the email? Mirror the greeting of the email in your reply.

In emails, people tend to use very short sentences or longer sentences consistently. In your response, match the sentence length in your own communication. Is the email all in one block of text, or are there spaces between each sentence? Pay attention to the structure when you write your response. Did he sign off with just his name? Did he use *sincerely* or *regards*? Match his salutation if it is a close match to what you would say naturally.

Learning the tools of psychology and using them effectively is an important part of being a real estate agent. However, with mirroring or any other technique described in this book, it should always be filtered through two overarching principles:

1. Is this something that will help my client?
2. Is this honest?

Maybe more than any other principle discussed in this book, mirroring can be used to manipulate people in disgusting ways. In fact, I debated whether I should even include this section but decided to keep it along with this word of warning to unscrupulous agents.

On a podcast I listened to recently, I heard an agent in an interview talking about some of the tactics he had used to become successful. He advocated using techniques that were unethical and manipulative of his clients, the kinds of things that give other agents a bad reputation.

In one example, he talked about going over to list a house and noticing that the older single lady he was interviewing had a pronounced limp. He immediately started limping with the same leg, and when she asked about it, he told her he'd always had knee trouble and would need surgery soon.

Was this effective? In the short term, it definitely was. He got the listing. However, when you look at this for what it really is, you see that it's a manipulative lie used to gain an advantage over an unsuspecting person. Don't ever use these tactics, or any others, to take advantage of someone else. Use them to put your best foot forward and to take note of ways you can improve your own natural skill set, but don't lie.

It won't matter how many listings or sales you get if you end up treating others as less than human, just cogs to be moved around in your real estate money-making machine. On this podcast, I could tell that the interviewers immediately became uncomfortable with the agent's techniques. He smugly let them know that the end justified the means. If you truly believe that you are the best agent, he said, then you should use any means, even dishonest ones, to gain clients.

Don't fall into the trap of believing your own hype. Treat people genuinely and build rapport with them honestly. There is zero need to lie to others to build rapport. Spend a little more time getting to know them, and you'll find dozens of ways to connect with them naturally, without sacrificing your own humanity.

How Am I Supposed to Do That?

Of all the techniques in Voss's *Never Split the Difference*, this next technique is my favorite for real estate. It's a great way to force the other agents to reveal more information than they want to and negotiate against themselves. Here is how it would look in a typical negotiation:

> Other agent: "My buyers are offering $120,000."
> You: "Ugh. We felt like we had it priced fairly. How are they supposed to accept $120,000?"

At this point, the usual response will reveal more information that you can use to aid your clients. For example, the other agent may say, "This is just the first offer," or he might mention that the dining room table your sellers were leaving is of no value to the buyers, so you can keep that. The point is to force the other agent to explain the price.

This technique also puts you on the same team as the other agent in that agent's mind. Sometimes, you can even ask, "How are we supposed to do that?" and allow the other agent to brainstorm ways to get the deal done and reveal even more information.

This also works for negotiations after the property is under contract. One example would be negotiating repairs after an inspection. Don't neglect these techniques just because you have an agreement. Until the property closes and keys are exchanged, you are always negotiating the best deal for your client. Whether you need to use this question after an agreement is reached because of the appraisal, inspections, or unexpected delays, it works.

Anchoring

One technique that master negotiators have used since the first marketplace opened is anchoring. In real estate, you usually get the chance to use this only if you're representing the buyers. Essentially, you should advise your clients to go in lower than they want to in most circumstances. You want to set a lower price in the seller's mind to anchor his expectations.

Think about a house listed for $100,000. If you offer $88,000 right off the bat, the sellers will, naturally, look at the offer as $12,000 less than list price and likely be dissatisfied. Now, if you make an offer at $70,000, and it's rejected, you can come back at $88,000. Suddenly the offer is $18,000 better than the last offer and looks more favorable.

Anchoring works. However, you have to be careful of two things. First, if there is a lot of competition, then this technique probably won't work. It works best if your clients are the only ones currently interested in the property. That said, sometimes you can play off someone else's anchor. If a listing agent reveals she had an offer but that it was a real lowball and didn't go anywhere, then your clients are already in a better position. Someone else has set an anchor for them, and if the sellers get another low offer, they will really rethink their pricing.

Second, you must be careful not to offend the sellers, especially if they're in a position not to sell if they don't want to. In my market, we often deal with luxury homes that are weekend or retirement places. When a seller lists a second home and has the option of waiting it out, it's hard to use this technique to get the price down.

What about when you represent the seller? Minimize the initial offer with your clients as much as you can if it is a lowball. Explain what the buyers are trying to do, respond nicely, and ask for another offer. Never think about the first offer again. Compare future offers only to the original listing price and not to previous lowball offers they have made. Anchoring works automatically, and you have to work against it for your client's best interest if you are representing the seller.

Body Language

I always try to present an offer in person. Voice inflection, tone, and body language make up more than 90 percent of communication, and if you just send offers via email, you lose the opportunity to see reactions firsthand and gather additional information. When you can, present the offer in person. When you can't, convey the offer verbally over the phone before sending it via email so that you can get an honest verbal reaction from the other agent.

Use any natural advantages you have when you negotiate. Giving an offer to another agent confidently can help your clients get a better price.

The Soft Counter

What do you do when there's an opportunity to add value for your clients, but an actual counter is not the best way forward? For example, the buyer might ask for an extension of a week to close. As an agent, your job is to get some value in exchange for a concession like this, but an exchange can be easier said than done.

If you submit an actual amendment asking for $2,000 in additional earnest money in exchange for the extension, what do you do if the buyer refuses to sign? Is the seller willing to walk away from the deal? At this point there is an impasse, and it can be hard for either side to back down completely. At the very least, it will cause unnecessary friction.

On the other hand, you also shouldn't just accept a contract concession without trying to get some value back for your client. That is a bad precedent to set, and if the deal ultimately falls through, you want your clients to be compensated for time lost while the property was under contract. It's possible the buyers are asking for an amendment to the original agreement as a stalling tactic for a more serious issue they aren't disclosing, and you can't be sure as an agent until the deal actually closes.

My favorite way to handle a situation like this is to use what I call a "soft counter." When you get a request for an extension or some other concession, try using this technique:

> Other agent: "My clients need to extend closing by a couple of weeks. They've had some family issues come up, and it can't be avoided."
> You: "Let me talk to my client and see what we can do, then I'll get back with you."

Confer with your client and explain the soft counter that you want to try. Let some time pass before you get back in touch with the other agent. As long as there's enough breathing room on the contract dates, I typically like to wait at least twenty-four hours.

> You: "I talked things over with my client, and she's thinking about it. Honestly, they're having a tough time with extending . . . just feeling nervous about this deal falling through and losing time that they could have spent on the market. I know your folks are solid, but it is a hard decision."

Other agent: "I know. We have to get this extension if we are going to close this deal. There's just no other way to make it happen right now."

You: "They're still talking it over and may need to sleep on it one more night. Do you think your folks would be willing to put up some more earnest money? Say $2,000? I think if that were the case, it would be a lot easier for my clients to swallow and get this done."

Other agent: "I'm not sure, but I'm happy to run it by them."

You: "Great! I think if we can get something like that, my clients will be ready to move on and we can get this done."

Notice what you have done using this technique. You haven't given an actual counter, which would mean a rejection of the original extension request and then a proposal of new terms. Instead, you have politely asked the buyers to change their offer to make it more palatable for the sellers. Nine times out of ten, you'll get them to make a better offer to your clients.

On the off chance you don't, you are still in a good position to get the deal done. Because you haven't actually countered, your sellers can still accept the proposed offer on the table and extend the closing if that makes the most sense for them.

The soft counter is a great way to stretch a contract during final negotiations as well, without having to actually counter and risk losing a deal. For instance, on a recent deal I closed, we had negotiated everything, but I felt like there was still a little more room for value for my clients. Before they signed the final offer, I got back in touch with the other agent.

They had requested that the refrigerator be left in exchange for $1, which is common in real estate transactions of this type. I told the other agent that I thought we had a deal, but would the buyer be willing to pay for the refrigerator? The sellers had their heart set on keeping it and that would make it easier for them to move forward. Say $500? Ten minutes later, the other agent texted me and said it was a deal.

Again, I did not submit an actual counter, but used a soft counter to try to create value for my clients. In this case it worked well, and my sellers were able to add $500 to their bottom line, a 10 percent bump on their profits.

Use the soft counter when you're about to finalize a contract or when you're already under contract and additional negotiations are needed. It's an effective tool that protects your client's downside while offering them a lot of upside as well. When I called my client and told them I was able to get them $500 more, they were very grateful. When you help your clients get real value in exchange for nothing, you show you're a professional negotiator who understands all the nuances of getting the best deal for your clients.

Never Agree to the First Offer

One mistake that real estate agents frequently make is to advise their sellers to accept the first offer without making any changes. What is the first thing that the buyers will think if they offer 80 percent of the purchase price and the seller agrees right away? They will think, "We should have come in lower."

In a real estate transaction, the buyer still has a lot of power during the contract phase in a typical deal. If they start off feeling like they could have purchased the property for less, the deal will be more likely to fall through. They will ask for too much money on repairs, find a reason they don't like it anymore, or come up with some other reason to get out of the contract and move on to something else.

Always find something to counter, especially on the first offer. If it's full price, find terms to counter. Ask them to pay for the survey, or instead of selling them the dining room set for $10 like they asked, charge them $500.

In very rare circumstances, you'll have a deal that is too good to pass on. In that case, I advise trying one of two things. First, you can try a soft counter and see what the buyers' agent says. Tell the other agent, "My seller loves the offer, but we also really wanted [fill in the blank]. Do you think the buyer would be open to that?" Notice that you didn't make a counter and lock your sellers into a new counter. Instead, you're just asking a question and telling them your sellers are still thinking about it.

If there isn't even room for a soft ask like that, you can always accept the offer, but verbally counter the other agent. Tell him, "My folks have accepted, but they really didn't want to. With the activity we have had so quickly, they feel like they underpriced it. I convinced them it was a good deal, but they won't be very negotiable on inspections or anything else."

The Ackerman Model
Negotiations should mostly focus on psychology and emotion because we make our decisions with our gut and not with our brain. Always keep that in the front of your mind when you're negotiating, no matter how frustrated, angry, or even elated you get. You can't stop your emotions from influencing your decisions, but you can be more aware of what you're feeling and how emotions may affect the outcome.

That said, the following is a very practical tool for negotiation that will come in handy as a real estate agent. I use this model myself when buying investment property, and it's often a good fit for negotiating deals for clients as well. It works best when there is little or no competition, just like any negotiating technique. This one takes some time to play out, but the result is a much better price.

The Ackerman model of negotiating has six rules, as explained in *Never Split the Difference:*[1]

1. Set your target price (goal). This is rarely the list price of a property; typically it will be lower.

2. Make your first offer at 65 percent of your target price. In other words, if the property is listed for $120,000 and your target is $100,000, offer $65,000. Remember, making a low offer like this sets an anchor with the other party. Even if they don't respond, you have shaped the conversation by putting the first number out there.

3. Calculate three rates of decreasing increments leading up to your goal (85 percent, 95 percent, 100 percent). In other words, on your second offer, you should raise the price by 20 percent of your target, then 10 percent of your target for your third response, and finally 100 percent of your target (in our example, that would be $85,000, $95,000, and $100,000).

4. Use different ways of saying no to get the other side to counter before increasing your offer. One of my favorite ways to get a response is to use the word *fair*. We made the offer, and we think it would be fair for the seller to give us a response. Or if they ask you to raise your offer first, you can ask, "How are we supposed to do that?" and put it back in their court. Review the rest of the negotiation section for other ideas.

5. When calculating your offers and raises, use specific numbers instead of round numbers. This is really easy to do and very effective. You will save your clients money simply by responding with numbers that sound firm. If you anticipate three or four rounds of negotiation before arriving at a price, save this technique for your last round or two. When you offer $99,876 instead of $100,000 even as your last counter, you are making it firm and showing the other party you are out of negotiating room.

6. Once you reach 100 percent, throw in a nonmonetary item. If you're representing a seller, you can use a piece of furniture. Again, this signals you're at the end of your negotiation and have

offered all you can. If you're a buyer, you can offer to pay for a small item on the contract, like the survey if one is necessary. You could also offer a letter at this point that explains other reasons why you want the property and show pictures of your client's family.

The Reverse Ackerman for Sellers

When you represent a seller, reverse the above process. The goal is to get the other party to pay as much as possible. I modified the Ackerman model so that I could use the best techniques for sellers as well as buyers.

1. When you receive your first offer on the property, make it uncomfortable for the other agent to give you a lowball number. Often when an agent submits an offer he's embarrassed by, he will try to avoid communication with you because he knows you will pick up on subtle clues. Make them present the offer to you in person if you can, or at least over the phone.

2. After you hear the number, you have a few options for response. My favorite is to use the fair question again and cause them to come up with reasons to support their number. No matter what number they say at first, you should take an audibly deep breath right after they say it, or gasp. Then follow that up with the following question or develop your own: "That number seems very low. My sellers really just want what's fair. How are they supposed to accept an offer like that?"

   The goal here is to get the other agent to counter right away in some capacity to give you some information to work with. Use the natural tension that comes when presenting a low offer and let the silence work its magic. You will be shocked at what other agents will tell you just to relieve the tension at this stage. I've had agents say, "Let me go back to my buyers again and make sure this is what we want to do," but even more often I've had agents convey that this was just a first offer and that there was definitely room to come up.

Notice that without doing anything, you have effectively countered at list price and forced the other party to clarify their position. Before you even get a chance to speak with your sellers, you have gathered a lot of information about where the other party stands and what kind of room they have to raise their offer.

3. Ideally, you want to counter the first offer at full price, just as I outlined above, and get the buyers to come back with a better price. Practice saying no without saying no, and explain to your sellers your reason for handling the negotiations this way. If that doesn't work, or if the other agent remains tightlipped and doesn't budge, then you can move on to the next step. Calculate the target price with your seller if you have not done so already, and then convert it to a percentage based on the list price. In other words, if your list price is $100,000 and your target is $90,000, then you have 10 percent negotiating room. Your percentage will change depending on the listing.

4. Again, plan for four rounds of negotiation, but this time as a seller. Here's how that looks:

   ⊚ After an initial offer, say no without saying no. This is effectively a full-price counter.

   ⊚ After you get the buyers to come up and if the price is not acceptable, drop the price by half of your calculated negotiating room. In the example we used above, that would mean dropping the price by 5 percent or $5,000.

   ⊚ When they respond, say no without saying no and try to get another counter out of them or at least more information.

   ⊚ When they give you another counter, drop the price by 25 percent of your total negotiation percentage budget. In the example, that would be $2,500.

   ⊚ After your response, repeat saying no without saying no to try to get them to respond.

- Drop the rest of the way to your price but be sure to end on a specific, odd number. Don't make your last counter $90,000, but rather $89,986.

- If they come back again and resist coming up, throw in one other item your sellers didn't want to keep—the refrigerator or the television hanging on the wall. The point is to let them know that financial negotiations are over and there is not much value left.

5. Keep in mind it's very rare to go through all these steps, whether you're representing the buyer or seller. Few agents, much less clients, have the stomach for protracted negotiations. Keep the ball moving and try to get the absolute best deal for your clients.

    One more thing: if you can help it, don't use any standard form that rejects the offer without giving a counter. In Texas, that form is called an Invitation to Resubmit. In my experience, these forms are clunky and tend to end the conversation rather than keep negotiations going. By rejecting the price in writing and telling the buyer to submit a new price, you are taking the lazy way out and will likely put an end to all negotiations. Instead of using the form, practice using the verbal counters discussed, and you will have more success.

The Ackerman model is an extremely effective tool that will give you a framework to build your negotiating system around. By building in set raises before you begin, you will help counteract any emotional decisions that your clients want to make when negotiating. Using this process should help you get the best price possible for your clients. Practice, practice, practice. Read *Never Split the Difference* once a year and try to read at least two other negotiation books each year as well.

Bonus Tip #11:

Giving small gifts, especially once you have a connection with a client, is vital to sustaining the relationship. If you close a deal with a buyer and she moves into her new house, she's going to make connections in the community and meet other agents quickly.

Give her a gift when you close. I like to give something that will introduce them to the area, like a gift certificate to a local restaurant they like. There is some benefit to giving a gift a week or two after the actual closing too. I will often go by the house and deliver it in person and check out what they've done with the place. This gives you another chance to interact with them, and it also puts you in their home after the sale.

Side note: I usually wait to ask my clients for an online review until this point as well. I've found it very effective to follow up with a gift and instructions on how to leave me a review. The client isn't moving anymore and has a little more time, but the sale is also recent enough that clients remember how much they valued what you did for them.

Throughout the year, you should keep up with this client through handwritten cards, calls, emails, and at minimum one gift per year. I give a dozen cookies from a local restaurant to all my clients every year, and that little act has turned into something many of them look forward to. If you're giving your clients even one gift a year, you are doing more than 90 percent of the other agents out there. When it comes time to list, you will get the listing.

If you don't give gifts and regularly keep in touch, you're asking for trouble. I often send thank-you gifts and cookies to clients that were represented by another agent in a transaction I was involved in. For example, if an agent represented a buyer on one of my listings, I often send the buyer a thank-you gift along with the rest of my clients. This is a nice way to welcome him to the area and show how I am different. If you aren't giving your clients gifts, another agent will. And they won't be your clients for long.

How to Always
Get a Full Commission

One of the hardest parts of being a real estate agent, especially when you're starting out, is learning how to handle commission objections. Almost every time you list a property, you'll be asked to cut your commission. You have to be ready to respond and fight for a full commission not only because you deserve it, but because it's often best for your client.

Don't believe me? Consider this: Would you be more motivated to sell a property on which you'll earn $10,000 in commission, or a property on which you'll earn only $5,000? We are all human, and whether we like it or not, money plays a part in our motivation.

The first thing you need to admit is that most agents don't deserve a full commission. Recognize that most agents should be discounting their commission because they aren't good at their job. It's perfectly reasonable for a client to ask you to cut yours before they have worked with you. The client expects the kind of service that deserves a reduced fee.

Work to show you're a different kind of agent right off the bat. Establish your expertise quickly, use testimonials to show social proof, and control the conversation with the listing tools that you've learned in this book. It's helpful to take a step back mentally when you hear an objection from a client and realize that most agents deserve a pay cut. Don't be one of those agents. Show that you are different right away and work to deserve full pay.

You should have a listing agreement already filled out when you go interview for a listing. Have your full commission in the appropriate blank (typed in, not inked in with pen). As you go through the listing with your client, fill in blanks that are left open—their contact information, exclusions to the improvements, and even the price.

When you get to the listing commission, just mention that your company charges that amount and move on. Often, having the commission already filled in like this and not addressing it as negotiable will be enough to head the conversation off so that you can avoid the discussion. Having a listing agreement filled out already is a must when you're meeting for a listing. You should also have the term of the listing filled out. The two most important things on a listing agreement besides price are term and commission, so try to take those off the negotiating table as much as possible.

Your client is more uncomfortable than you are when talking about commission. When the conversation comes up—and it often will even if you prove your value up front and have the listing filled out—what do you do next? Keep in mind that he is more uncomfortable than you are. Almost nobody likes to talk about money or how much someone else gets paid, but at the same time there is an obligation to try to negotiate for as much as possible. Don't rush through the commission objection. Pause and take your time, use the tension to your advantage, and don't be afraid of the conversation.

Most agents will quickly agree to anything a client asks to get the listing and resolve the tension. Don't be tempted to do the same. Take your time when you're asked to lower your commission, try to understand your client's point of view, and don't be afraid to push back.

There are many reasons you should not lower your commission, and when a client asks you to lower it, it's time to bring those reasons up. Don't bring up support for your commission until after the client has asked for this, because ideally you want to avoid the conversation completely. Below are some of the reasons I offer:

- I'm a full-service real estate agent, so I don't discount our fees.
- We use professional photographers, have a great website, and pay for advertising in multiple places. I promise I'm not just going to throw a picture up online and walk away.
- I have many other listings already, and it would not be fair to them to change my listing commission for one client. I have already committed to them.
- The standard buyer's commission is 3 percent in this area. It's in your best interest to offer a full-price commission, because we don't want to financially influence other agents to promote another property over yours.
- I have similar listings that are offering a full-price commission. I don't want to be put in a position of getting paid less for yours because I want to be sure to offer you the same level of service.
- Use a question to put the commission objection back in their court. Ask, "How am I supposed to lower my commission and still offer you full service?" When you ask this, stop talking. It may take your clients a while to support what they've asked. Listen to their reasoning and address it appropriately.

Sometimes you have to deal with another listing agent that you're in competition with who's already offered to lower his commission. This objection deserves a special mention because you'll get it more often than any other objection. Remember there are many agents who don't deserve a full commission, and many others too cowardly to fight for what they deserve, so this should not be a surprise. Prepare to handle this objection, and you'll be ready when the time comes. Here's my favorite response:

"That's interesting. It seems like he offered to discount his commission pretty quickly. Let me ask you a question: If he's that willing to give away the money in his own pocket, how hard do you think he's going to fight for your money during negotiations?"

This usually doesn't end the conversation, but it defines the rest of it. You appropriately framed the other agent as a discount real estate agent who isn't very professional. Then you can use the other reasons for not lowering your commission to support your own stance. This technique is extremely effective when used correctly. It's a great opportunity to separate yourself from the competition and show your professionalism.

Along the same lines, another similar objection you'll hear often is that they have another realtor who discounts his commission because he's involved in multiple transactions with the client. Your client will ask if you're willing to do the same. This happens quite a bit with investors who buy and sell a lot of properties. I point out that I work with other investors who offer a full commission on both buying and selling, and I want to bring deals to everyone on equal footing. Obviously, if someone is paying me more on both ends, he will get priority. If you have established yourself as a valuable real estate agent who offers a lot of value, this will work.

Even after offering great reasons for not lowering your commission, there will be times when you have to offer something to get the deal done. Here is the best way you can offer a concession without giving up much commission: offer to discount the commission if you are the only agent involved. I say something like this: "How about this: if I happen to be the only agent involved, I will discount my commission from 6 percent to 5 percent. Does that sound fair?"

Most of the time when you reach this stage in the conversation, that's all it will take. Most people want to be done and move on from the conversation to actually get their property sold. And as nice as it is to be the only agent involved in a transaction, it doesn't happen that often. In my experience, this is an easy concession to make that rarely changes your bottom line.

In the rare case they refuse your proposal, you have a few options on how to proceed. Most importantly, decide what you're willing to do with each individual property before you get to this point so that you won't end up making a poor decision you have to live with for six to twelve months.

Ask yourself two questions before moving forward on the commission question. First, "Is the property sellable at the price and terms you have already settled on?" If the answer is an honest yes, then it may make sense to discount your commission slightly more depending on the property. If the answer is no, ask yourself, "Will this property attract new clients for my business, whether buyers or sellers?" Sometimes you will come across a property that is a tough sell, but it's a great bait property that will help you reel in buyer prospects and sell them on other places. It's important to be honest with your client about what you think the true market value and a reasonable selling time are, but on the other hand you need to weigh all the factors when making a decision about listing. This is especially true for a listing when you're about to discount your commission.

If the answer to both of the questions above is no, don't discount your commission. In fact, you should consider walking away even if they offer to sign at a full commission. There are no reasons I am aware of to list a property if it's not marketable and won't attract other clients.

You have to be willing to walk away from the table and let them list with someone else. Clients will be able to tell if you are willing to sign absolutely anything, and some of them will take advantage of you for this. Be willing to stand up, shake hands, and wish them good luck. Someone who is that worried about a half a percent on their commission is going to be a huge pain to deal with anyway; you may have dodged a bullet.

Many times, at this point you'll find out they've been bluffing, that the other real estate agent who offered to discount his commission 2 percent is actually their third cousin who lives seven hours away. You may be called back to the table quickly.

If you have to discount a commission because it's just too good of a deal to pass up, that's fine. There are definitely times to do that. But be aware that if you are setting a precedent, it may be hard to change in the future. Be honest with yourself about what the compromise means for both your current business and your future business so that you can weigh all the costs appropriately.

By now, you have a signed listing agreement for either a full commission or a reasonable discount based on your own decision, or you've walked away and wished them luck. In any scenario, you should feel good about the process you just went through. Arguing for a fair commission is part of your job as a professional agent, and when you don't ask for what you're worth, you're hurting yourself, your family, and the entire profession.

Always remember that getting a full commission is often best for your clients as well. This can be hard to explain because many don't trust real estate agents, but the reality is that if selling Home A brings less money for the agent then selling Home B, the agent will be more inclined to point clients toward Home B. Don't allow your clients to save a few pennies when there are dollars on the line, or you're doing them a disservice.

The First Two Laws of Real Estate

The Law of Never Cutting Your Commission
An easy way to get listings—and a fast way to race to the bottom—is to cut your commission to beat out other real estate agents. It could be worth hundreds of thousands of dollars over the course of your real estate career to learn the above techniques and secure a full commission.

Many agents assume they're doing favors for friends by offering a discount, or at least walking away with some commission versus no commission. Don't buy into it. I have used the commission objection techniques above with multiple sellers and been able to turn a higher commission into a positive rather than a negative when compared with other agents.

Of course, there are exceptions to this rule, but they are very rare and don't come up more than once a year. Fight for your commission and serve your clients better. After all, if you aren't protecting your value, will you protect theirs?

The Law of Fiduciary Responsibility
This law falls along the same lines of the previous, but it's worth thinking through. As agents, we have a fiduciary responsibility to put our clients' interests first. This can easily be overlooked, and I have found that agents often get this wrong. Rather than put their clients' fiduciary interests first, they put their own fiduciary interests *last*. That is not the same thing.

To put your clients' interests first is not admitting that they are opposed to your own interests. In fact, if you are a good agent and doing what you're supposed to do, your clients' fiduciary interests and your own should be closely aligned. If you are the best agent, a full-service agent who treats clients ethically, fights for their bottom line, and always communicates with them clearly, then you have a responsibility to be selfish when it comes to your own financial interests. Again, you won't be as focused on their property if you aren't being paid fair value. That hurts your clients' interest; it does not help them.

Commit to continually improve as an agent. Build your knowledge base, hone your negotiating skills, follow up after sales, and learn everything you can about this business. To align your interests with your clients' so that you both make more money, you have to give them the quality of service you're being paid for. When you compromise and put your fiduciary interests in opposition to your clients', you are often doing them a disservice.

At times, there will be tension between your interests and theirs. In these cases, your clients always come first. One example I have run into is showing someone a property I end up liking as well. You have a responsibility in that case to make it clear that, if the client passes, you are interested in it; then show the client all the reasons you think it's a good deal. Again, your interests should grow to be more aligned with your clients' as you continue in the real estate business.

Customers vs. Clients

Do you know the difference between a customer and a client? In just one transaction, knowing the difference and being able to explain it effectively earned me $90,000 in commission. Here's what you should know.

A client is someone that you represent as an agent, that you have a fiduciary responsibility to, and that you will work to get the best deal for. This is the traditional agent relationship and one you should be familiar with already. Learn the responsibilities, study the codes of ethics in your state, and take this representation very seriously.

A customer is someone you are working with but who is not a client. This means you aren't representing him or her as an agent. You can still provide excellent service, but you must let the customer know that your primary responsibility lies with your clients.

I had a property listed, about six hundred acres. After showing another listing to a prospect, I recommended he come and look at this one because I thought it would be a better fit. He ended up loving it and decided to write an offer. I explained that as the listing agent, I could not represent him as a client but would happily take him on as a customer as long as he knew my primary responsibility was to my client.

On a transaction that size, lawyers get involved. The buyer's lawyer had a problem with me being the only agent involved, so I had to explain the difference between a customer and a client, even going so far as to send them information on the difference from my state's real estate commission. Fighting for a large commission like this while keeping the deal together was like threading a needle, but it worked. The lawyers finally understood, and we moved forward.

One more thing: the buyer I took on as a customer was a licensed real estate broker. He chose to use me because I brought him the property and worked with him. He did this even though it cost him close to $100,000 in commission. That lesson taught me a couple of things. First, when you really know what you're doing as a professional, it's worth a lot of money—probably more than you realize. It's worth paying for the right kind of representation in certain circumstances, even if you're an agent.

Second, it never hurts to ask. When it was time to write the contract, I asked if he wanted me to draw up the paperwork and take him on as a customer, even though he was an agent. My favorite quote from Timothy Ferriss in *The 4-Hour Workweek* applies here: "Success can be measured in the number of uncomfortable conversations you are willing to have."[1]

Knowing small pieces of information and being able to communicate them effectively can be rewarding. Learn what it takes to be an agent and what it really means, and you will find opportunities that can reward you. Knowing the difference between a customer and a client never seemed that valuable to me, until it was. If you wait to know your business until crunch time, then it may be too late.

Bonus Tip #12:

Learn to see others' problems in new ways and identify problems they didn't know they had. Real estate has shifted from a business that controlled all the access to information to one that is all about solving problems. Twenty years ago, there was very little information parity; prospects and clients had to rely on agents to even know which properties were listed. Now the role of the agent is to help curate the massive amount of information available to clients and to help them clarify exactly what they want.

Think about your own real estate business and how you can use this principle. At the first meeting, I often give clients a tour of my area and point out different neighborhoods I think would fit their needs. I can help them clarify exactly what they are looking for long term by doing this, and often what they thought they wanted at the beginning of the day will have shifted by the end of the day.

Don't be a walking version of Google or Zillow, just regurgitating the information anyone can get online. If someone asks you about a home you have seen, tell her how you felt when you were there, what sounds you heard, what the drive in was like, what neighbors are nearby, whether it's a good investment for the future, and anything else personal you can think of. Don't just give the lot size and the number of bathrooms that the house has. Your client can find that information easily, and you have to move way beyond the basic facts to have anything useful to offer.

Three Closing Techniques

There is a lot of bad, outdated advice on how to close a real estate transaction. As an agent committed to helping clients make the best decision, you must always keep in mind that your clients' interests come first. Help them push past their own resistance at times, but don't use manipulation and power games to convince them to sign something they aren't ready for.

Think of yourself as a consultant, someone to help guide your clients to the best decisions. You're not selling properties; you're selling yourself as the best person to help your client buy or sell a property.

These are the three closing techniques I use 95 percent of the time: **the Option Close, the Draft Contract Close, and the Financing vs. Cash Close.** The sections below detail each of these techniques, including sample scripts of exactly how I use them.

The Option Close

As in most other states, Texas has a buyer's option built into the contract. This option allows buyers to perform due diligence and make sure the house is a fit for them. They have the option to get out of the contract within an agreed upon time frame, usually a week or two, for a nominal amount of money, rarely more than a few hundred dollars. Here is an example of how the conversation goes using this technique:

Agent: "I know that it's been a while since you bought or sold a property. Are you familiar with the option period, or did you use it in the past?"

Client: "No, what is that?" (In my experience, the answer is almost always no. It really doesn't matter if it's yes or no, though; you can continue the same way with some minor tweaks.)

Agent: "It's a great way to lock down a property while you think about it and continue getting your questions answered. When you write a contract, you ask the seller for a two-week option period. It's always negotiable, but typical for this area is about two weeks for $100. During this time, you can get inspections, meet contractors, talk to your other family members, and really make sure this is the right place for you. At any time during the option period, for any reason, you can notify the seller that you are opting out and get out of the contract. Your earnest money is protected and will be returned, so all you would lose is the $100 and any additional money you spend on the inspections. You can literally get out of the contract for any reason. If you wake up on the wrong side of the bed one day, you can opt out and you don't even have to give a reason."

Client: "Wow, that sounds like a great tool. What would I have to do to start that process?"

Agent: "Well, the option doesn't start until both parties agree on a contract. We could fill out an offer and present it to the sellers. Assuming they accept it, we'll also need two checks: the earnest money for the title company, and the option money for the seller. During the option, the buyer has all the power. No one else can put the property under contract. If you discover any issues on inspection, you have leverage to get the price lowered, but the seller does not have the same option to get out of the contract like you do."

Client: "I can do that. If it's just going to be $100, I'm ready to try and see what happens."

Notice how much you've accomplished with just a short conversation about contract details. You've shifted your client's mindset from thinking about the price of the property to the price of the option period. You have allowed him some space to make a more informed decision, shifting the true decision date to a couple of weeks in the future. You've given him confidence he can get more answers inexpensively in the near future.

This is by far the most powerful closing technique I use, and it's hugely beneficial for clients. For some reason, many agents prefer to use high-pressure sales strategies. In my experience, this is the best way to get someone to take the next step, especially when you sense he really likes the property but is unsure what to do.

Explain that the next step is truly just a baby step in the right direction. Don't let your clients think that they're about to spend $300,000 and sign up to buy a house that day, because that's what they'll think by default. Instead, show them the right way to think about the next step—it's just a small investment to buy some time to make a more well-informed decision.

Once someone has made an offer and has an option on a property, it's very likely he will move forward and find a way to actually close it. Once someone has committed, even if it's a small amount of money, he usually finds a way to follow through on that commitment. Use this closing technique only when your client is ready and the property is a great fit for his needs. You will reap the benefits of being an enormous help to your client.

The Contract Draft Close

Another closing technique I use is the contract draft close. This is an easy way to ask a buyer if he's ready to write an offer on a property and ease him into it. This stage usually follows a great showing. Many times, you can use this when the buyer finds a good property earlier than expected and is unsure whether to keep looking or jump on it.

Here is a script for how it might sound, based on my experience:

> Buyer: "Wow, that was a great fit for us. Did not expect to find a property so soon that met so many of our needs."
>
> Agent: "It was a great property—better than I expected too! I think it's a really good deal and may not last long. If it's one you like that much, it may be worth writing up an offer on it."
>
> Buyer: "I'm not sure we're quite ready to do that. It feels too early in the process, and we would like to look at a few more. Maybe we'll sleep on it and get back to you tomorrow."
>
> Agent: "I understand. Since it's been a while since y'all purchased a place, why don't we at least draw up a draft of an offer so you'll have it to look over? That will help your discussion and thought process tonight as you think it over."
>
> Buyer: "Great idea."

Drawing up a draft of an offer with clients is a great way to help them see how serious they really are. More often than not, the buyer will realize during the draft process that they really want the property. I've even had buyers who decide to sign and present the offer right away after going through the draft, because once the contract is understood, it's not the giant step forward that they were worried about. Going through the draft is also a great way to explain the different protections built into a contract for a buyer. The three largest protections are as follows:

The Option Period

Typically, the option period works better on a place with improvements than on raw land, but it is still the ultimate tool for buyers. Your buyers should understand that once the contract is accepted and the option money is given to the seller, they can opt out for any reason during the option period and just lose their option money. During the option period, the buyers have all the power because they can get out of the agreement at a very low cost.

Financing

On most contracts involving a loan, there are protections based on financing built into the contract. Your buyers should understand that if the property does not appraise or if they can't qualify for the loan terms they are seeking, then they can get out of the contract, and their earnest money will be protected. Many buyers don't fully understand this clause and want to wait until they talk with their bank, but with this protection in place, it may make sense to jump on in and write the contract.

Warning: if the shoe is on the other foot, and you're representing the seller, beware of the buyer's agent who lists unreasonable loan terms to give their buyers more protection. If someone says he's seeking a forty-year loan on a house at less than 2 percent interest, you can be sure he's not going to get it. Since the period for securing financing is typically longer than the option period, if your seller signs something that just won't ever work in the real world, then you're giving the buyer a free option period for a much longer amount of time.

Objection Period

The objection period is used for objecting to any new disclosures about the property that come up during the course of the contract. This can include new information that the survey reveals, the title commitment, or any other documents that have not been previously disclosed. The objection period is a very important tool for farm and ranch real estate, which I specialize in, because of the mineral ownership laws in Texas.

With the objection period, you have to be sure you object in writing as prescribed by the contract. Typically, at that point, the seller will have a certain number of days to cure the objection to the buyer's satisfaction. If that doesn't happen, the buyer will then have the option to request a release of earnest money because the duties of the seller were not met according to the contract. The buyer can also decide to move forward despite objections not being satisfied, should they choose to.

If you are the buyer's agent, be sure that on the initial draft of the offer you watch for any documents that are disclosed prior to the contract. There is a space to show any recorded documents that have already been disclosed. If documents have been previously disclosed, they are precluded from being objected to. If you have not been provided any documents, make sure nothing is listed there.

On the other hand, if you're representing the seller and you have provided recorded documents to the buyer for review before the contract, make sure you list them. If you have already disclosed the recorded easement for a pipeline, you don't want that to be an objection the buyers can bring up to get out of the contract without losing their earnest money should they change their mind later.

Drawing up a draft of an offer is a great exercise for both the buyer and the agent to go through. Talking through each point in a low-pressure setting is very useful for discovering what is truly important for your clients and for the particular property they're interested in.

The Contract Draft Close for Sellers

I use a version of this technique to close listings as well. In fact, I use this close for listings more often than I use it for purchase contracts because in most cases when representing a buyer, the option close works best. The option close is not a technique you can use with sellers, so this is the next best thing.

When you go to a listing appointment, have a listing agreement already filled out with all the information needed, except for price. As you go through your presentation, there will come a point when you need to push it one step further. With experience, you will know whether it's time to leave them the information to decide on later or time to push for a signed listing now. Either way, you should have a listing filled out.

Here's how it works:

> Seller: "Thanks for telling us about your company and what you'll do. It's very helpful to understand all the ins and outs.
> Agent: "Glad I could help! I also have a listing agreement I would like to go over with you here. We can go through it line by line and make sure that you don't have any other questions."
> Seller: "Okay, that will be great."

As you go through, explain each portion of the listing agreement. By this time, you should have already presented your price and term recommendations. I prefer to have my commission already filled in because it doesn't give them an additional opportunity to try to negotiate it. By the time you finish going through the agreement, they should have a great understanding of what they would be signing up for and also feel like they have taken ownership of the document because of their input.

At this point, you have a couple of options. Typically, if someone is close to making a decision right then, I will use humor to make it easier to say yes or give them a way to say no comfortably.

> Agent: "All right, I think that's everything. Did you have any other questions?"
>
> Seller: "No, I think this covers all that we had. Thank you!"
>
> Agent: "You're welcome. You know, it would be really easy for us both to sign this agreement right now. Then I can get started on the real work. Wouldn't it be nice to cancel those other interviews with the agents you have scheduled?"

This works right away maybe 20 percent of the time, and it's a very nice feeling when it does. If it doesn't work, don't worry about it. You have put yourself in a great position and answered all questions. Of all the listing appointments I've done in which I could view what other agents had presented, no one else has ever brought a listing agreement along with them. It's a very easy way to stand out, show your attention to detail, and act like a professional.

Financing vs. Cash Close

The majority of the time, I use the first two closes we covered. However, sometimes neither one quite fits. When that's the case, I often use the Financing vs. Cash close. The most common time I use this close is when I'm working with a buyer interested in a larger tract of land.

The thinking behind this close is simple. There are loans and lenders that you should become very familiar with to help settle your clients when they're on the fence. Because I work in a luxury market in which people often pay cash or think about paying cash, I've become familiar with land loans that may offer advantages over a cash offer.

Don't worry if you don't work in an area with raw land—you can also use this close by comparing local banks to national banks. Anytime creativity or speed is called for, this close can also be effective.

Here is how it may play out with raw land:

Buyer: "Wow, this is nicer than we thought it would be. It really has a lot going for it."

Agent: "Absolutely. Not too many pieces of land have all these features together. Were y'all thinking about paying cash or trying to get financing for this?"

Buyer: "We'll be paying cash." (It really doesn't matter whether they answer cash or loan; you can continue either way.)

Agent: "That's great. You know, I've had clients before who planned to pay cash, but after learning about land loans, they decided to go the financing route. Have you heard of ag financing for land through mutual companies?"

Buyer: "I don't think so."

Agent: "It has some real advantages over cash, and by the time you calculate the interest rate, it sometimes makes more sense to get a loan than pay cash." (At this point, go over more specific details of the loan programs you're familiar with.)

That's it. It's an easy conversation that offers valuable information on a loan that could save the buyer a significant amount of money. If the interest rate is low enough or the terms attractive enough, it often makes more sense for buyers to get a loan rather than pull cash out of other investments too quickly. This kind of insight will separate you from other agents.

Notice that by using this technique, you've shifted the conversation. Instead of talking about whether they're going to buy the property, you're talking to them about how best to purchase the property. Often just this subtle shift can help buyers make a decision faster because they're getting answers to many of their questions without having to face extra resistance.

You can use a similar technique for pitching a local bank over a national bank. Instead of asking about cash versus financing, ask if the buyer has decided whom to get a loan through. At this point, you can explain the differences between going local or national. Here is a short list of the advantages of using a local bank (in most areas):

- Local banks are easier to work with.
- Local banks are familiar with the unique area and special circumstances.
- Local banks can often be more flexible and creative.
- If you live in the area, there are huge advantages to building up a relationship with a local bank.
- Local banks are often able to close faster with less hassle.
- Yes, local banks often have higher interest rates than national banks. Be sure to weigh the other factors as well before making your decision.

As a real estate agent, you are a local entrepreneur. I really enjoy promoting local businesses, and most of the time I believe that working with a local bank will offer your client many more advantages over the long haul. It's not always easy to help people see past the interest rate, but regardless of whether they choose local or national, this is a great conversation to have and a good way to close.

As you talk about which bank to use or whether to use cash versus financing, it's very easy to transition to the paperwork. If you sense the client isn't quite ready to do that, you've still set up a very easy way to follow up by talking about financing. Introduce them to the banks that you've pitched to them and let the loan programs and lenders speak for themselves.

These conversations are a very effective way to get people to consider an offer more seriously. With this closing technique and the two others before it, you are portraying yourself as a tremendously valuable agent to your client while also subtly asking the hardest question: "Are you ready to buy this property?"

These closing techniques have been very fruitful for me, but don't be afraid to come up with your own as you learn your local market and see what works best with your personality. The important thing is to figure out a way to ask a low-stakes question about the contract that will offer value to your client and also give you important information about what the next step should be. Don't be afraid to ask the tough question, but remember that thinking through the best way to ask it is part of your job as a real estate agent.

Bonus Tip #13:

Pay your taxes with every commission. There is no bigger mistake that new agents make after a closing than not setting enough money aside for taxes. Get ready, because taxes for agents are no joke. Put 30 percent of your commissions in a separate account as soon as they come in. When tax time comes, you'll be prepared, and you won't have to think about it. Hopefully you'll have some left over in your tax account to start next year off right too. I am not an accountant and don't have any great tricks on saving taxes, but here are a few things I do:

- *Use your day planner to track where you're going. I don't keep track of miles (does anybody really do that?), but I do have a record of everywhere I go each day. Write-offs for mileage and travel will really add up.*

- *Get a separate credit card for your business expenses. I put all gas, marketing, client gifts, and other incidentals on one card, making it very easy to create itemized worksheets at the end of the year.*
- *Do your own taxes. At least try this your first few years in real estate. It's not that hard, and it will help show you what you're missing and how much you really pay in taxes. I've grown to value paying taxes myself because it hurts so much. When payment gets taken out each month, you forget what you're losing. Feeling the sting will help you make better decisions.*

Searching for the Best Clients

When you first start out in real estate, you should jump at any chance to work with just about any client. You need to learn as much as possible in a short amount of time, so pick up the scraps that others in your office don't want to deal with. I used to work at the office during floor time and wait for the other agents to leave for lunch so I could have a chance of getting a call during the lunch hour.

After you've worked with clients for a while, you'll realize that the 80/20 rule applies to clients as well as agents. Detailed in an earlier chapter on agents, the 80/20 rule in business states that 80 percent of the output usually results from 20 percent of the input. In this case, 80 percent of your income will be generated by just 20 percent of your clients. And they may not be the first clients you think of.

- Recent clients (especially buyers). You'll be surprised at how many people change their minds after they buy a property. Many times, job situations change faster than expected, they decide the house is not a fit, or they just like to move. Your recent clients can be some of your most valuable clients.
- Investors. They buy and sell properties more often, and once you establish yourself with them, you can grow a profitable relationship. You can build your entire business on just one investor if you get the right one.

- Clients looking for more expensive property. Of course, the price of a property will increase your commission, so you should definitely give more weight to clients in a higher price range.

The above list can also be summarized as RFM. Perry Marshall, a marketing expert, uses this tool to help determine which clients are in the 20 percent.[1] The RFM tool stands for Recency, Frequency, and Money. Here's how you can use it in real estate:

- Create a list of all your clients, preferably in a spreadsheet.
- For each client, rate her recency on a scale of 1 to 10. How recently has she worked with you? Communicated with you? The 1 to 10 is somewhat arbitrary, but as you go through each of these three determining factors, you'll get a sense for how each client should be rated.
- For each client, rate his likely frequency in the future. In other words, is this a client who will just buy and sell his primary home, or is he an investor who will buy ten properties a year? If you sell to someone you're pretty sure won't sell for the next twenty years, he should be a 1, while a very frequent investor should be a ten.
- Rate each client's price range on a scale of 1 to 10. If someone is just looking at a $60,000 home, he should probably be a 1. If she's looking for a $10 million commercial building, she should be closer to a 10.
- Take the three numbers for each of the three factors, add them up, and put them in a new column. Each client now has a number representing his or her RFM total, which should give you the baseline information you need to determine the top 20 percent of your clients.

The 20 percent should jump off the page when you finish this exercise, and this information can give you valuable insight on your current clients and whom you should focus on in the future as you grow your business. **The RFM tool is one of the most valuable exercises you can use as a real estate agent to learn where your efforts should be concentrated.**

Don't make the mistake of not working with those who don't make the top of the list or treating them as less valuable. If they're your clients, they should receive the top level of service you can provide regardless of their RFM score. But as you grow your business, you won't be able to work with everyone. There's only so much time in a day. The best way to use this tool is to figure out whom to focus on with your marketing efforts and whom to refer to another agent if necessary.

One kind of client I frequently refer to other agents is a primary home seller moving out of state. It's very unlikely he or she will move back to the area, making the frequency score far from the top 20 percent. Refer this kind of client to newer agents so that you can focus on clients with a higher RFM score.

If you don't have too many clients yet, ask experienced agents to refer some of these clients to you. You have to prove you will keep up with the leads you get and take great care of them. I only refer to other agents who are as dedicated as I am to providing a great level of service. At every stage, you should commit to providing your client a high level of service, no matter what. That may require you to refer a number of clients to work with someone else in your office if you don't have the time to give them your best.

Use the RFM model to quickly see who your best clients are and who you should be marketing to as well. This one tool could easily triple your income over the next few years if used correctly. Don't pass it by without careful consideration.

Qualifying Questions

"What is your timeline for purchasing a property?"

This is one of the first and best questions that I ask when I first meet buyers looking for property. You'll quickly learn from their answers how serious to take them and how high a priority to give them. If their answer is that they have already been looking for the perfect place for six years and haven't found it, they're probably going to be a waste of your time.

"What price range would you like me to stay under as I search for property?"

This question is great because you aren't asking what they can afford but what they want. This makes it easy for them to answer without feeling like they have to justify their answer. It's usually a red flag when someone is looking at a wide range of places with very different prices. They'll likely either lowball or be more of a tourist than an actual buyer.

Never Ask This Common Question

There is one question I never ask, even though every real estate agent that I've worked with does. If I get a call on one of my listings, or even just a call into our office, I never ask, "Are you already working with another agent?" Real estate gurus will tell you that should be the first question you ask, because you don't want to waste your time on someone who won't work with you. That's a mistake and here's why:

- Clients rarely understand an agent relationship. With many clients looking online today, buyers' representation agreements are signed less frequently. Working with an agent can mean many things, and I never assume that it means a definite agreement with another agent.
- Often at first contact, clients overemphasize that they've already seen property with someone. This is a defense mechanism, meant to guard against overaggressive salesmen. Let them use this defense strategy to feel more at ease, but don't assume it means you're out of the picture.
- Show value right away, however you need to do it. I often answer questions about the property and follow up with other

suggested properties and some material on choosing an agent, investing in real estate in our area, and other resources.

- If you know of a pocket listing, use it. Often when you first start working with someone, he will say he wants to work only with listing agents for a while. One easy way around this is to show them a pocket listing another agent has (so there would be no way for you to represent the seller, but also no way for the buyer to know about it without you telling them—thus, they need to use you as the buyer's agent). You can also use this technique on pre-listings coming up in your office. Bottom line: show them as many properties as you can right away.

- The worst-case scenario at this point is that you show a few listings to someone who ends up buying with someone else, and you lose out on a commission. This will happen to you, but far more often you will win the client over and end up representing him. Play the odds and work with anyone regardless of what he or she tells you at first contact.

Embrace the challenge of winning people over, and you'll be surprised at how effective you can be when you enter a conversation and a showing with a great attitude, willing to help no matter what. I've even won over real estate agents who wanted to represent themselves using this method, and they end up paying me to represent them even though representing themselves would save thousands of dollars. Don't buy into the lie that it's a waste of time to talk to a prospect who's already seen a property with another agent.

Bonus Tip #14:

Avoid temporary leases like the plague. Here are a few of the many nightmares that can happen when you allow a temporary lease:

1. *The new buyer breaks something in the house but claims it was already broken. Seller is on the hook. We've had this happen before with $12,000 worth of air-conditioning units.*
2. *The buyer has a chance to get cold feet and change his mind.*
3. *The house burns down or floods during the temporary lease, and the responsible party had not paid for insurance. This is a nightmare situation even if no one gets hurt and there is insurance in place.*
4. *There was an incident in our area in which the buyers were going to buy furniture from the seller at closing, but moved in early on a temporary lease. They moved in, skipped out of town a couple of nights later with a lot of expensive furniture, and canceled payment on their checks.*
5. *If it falls through for some weird reason, you have to find a way to kick them out. This can be harder than it sounds. Usually someone who needs a place to rent for just two or three weeks doesn't have anywhere else to go.*

Bottom line: Don't do it unless you absolutely have to.

Common Contract Issues

Sometimes contracts don't unfold as planned. As an agent, you have to figure out a way to keep them together. In this chapter, I'll address three common issues that crop up after a contract is in place and give you some tools for dealing with each situation below.

It's common for problems to arise in appraisals. I had an issue recently on a house that under appraised. This can happen for many reasons, but it's important to remember that appraisers are much more limited than real estate agents when determining value. Depending on the bank they're working for, they can often use only comparable properties that sold in the past twelve months in a small geographic area. Sometimes this approach and the comparable sales approach used by agents with a wider search area and timeline don't exactly line up.

First, you need to talk to your clients and figure out their main goal. Ideally at this point, you can go to the sellers and ask them to lower the price to match the appraisal. If they agree, then you're done, and your client has saved money.

This often won't work, but it's always worth a try. There are many reasons a property can under appraise, and the agent representing the seller will likely push back on requests for a price reduction as a first solution. You should do the same if you're representing the seller.

If you can't get the price lowered, then the next step is to read the appraisal. You will need to have your client give the bank permission for you to see it. Check the square footage of the subject home first. On one of my deals, the square footage was wrong, and correcting it fixed the problem. If that looks okay, read the rest of the report. What comparable sales did they use? Are there better options to use instead? If so, requesting that they use another property or explaining why they didn't is a great way to have them take a second look at the appraisal.

If they go back to the drawing board and are able to fix the appraisal, then great! If they can't make it happen for whatever reason, then you have to figure out an equitable way forward for all parties. I suggest splitting the difference at this point if your clients can bring the extra cash to closing to cover the difference in appraisal value, but only do this if you and your clients believe the property is worth more than the appraised value.

If you can't get the price lowered and you think that the appraisal is the correct valuation, it's best to walk away and find another property. Keeping a deal together for no good reason is not the right way to go. Move on to the next one if that's the case.

Inspections are probably the biggest reason why contracts fall apart. When a buyer brings in an inspector and has him go over the house with a fine-tooth comb, the inspector will find things wrong. Dealing with inspections in the right way is a key part of keeping contracts together.

Direct your clients to good inspectors. I know many agents who recommend poor inspectors who will rubber-stamp a house as good just to get the deal closed. This is a huge disservice to your clients, and while it may help you keep the deal together without any friction, this practice will catch up with you.

Instead, direct your clients to the toughest inspectors, the ones who will find absolutely everything wrong with the home. Explain to your client what the report will look like before he gets it, that it will be fifty pages of problems with the home, and that it's exactly what they need. I always try to present inspections as an investment, and with the inspectors I use, it almost always is. A $500 inspection can help you lower the purchase price of the property by $5,000, and that kind of return on investment is a real financial benefit for your client.

When you negotiate repairs, always ask for cash or a price reduction instead of repairs. Sellers might make temporary repairs on a house they're leaving in a few weeks to get the house in good condition to close. However, the buyers' goal is to have problems fixed permanently because it benefits them and because they don't want the same issues to surface whenever they sell the house. Push for monetary consideration and advise your clients not to accept repairs unless there is a very good reason.

Last, don't let buyers and sellers talk to each other until you get to the closing table. There is rarely anything good that comes of it, and it often brings a whole lot of headaches. My first year in real estate, I was working with a buyer who wanted to purchase another listing in our office. Circumstances came up that prevented that agent from communicating with the sellers, so I happily passed some things along. It was a complicated property, and the buyers naturally had a lot of questions. How do you work the aerobic septic system? What did you use the third house for? Why is there a giant bear in a cage in the middle of your property (for real)?

I naively put them in touch, and through a series of escalating issues, it created a problem. It was much harder for my clients to recognize the value I brought to the table when they were talking to the sellers directly, and small problems became big ones without my knowing it.

On closing day, the sellers came in with another agent and a lawyer. They had decided that they weren't going to pay us our commission. I was in over my head. I can still remember feeling like I was reeling from being punched and not knowing what to do. Fortunately, the listing agent was much more experienced and also owned our company, so he took over and negotiated what would happen.

I'd never had a closing like that before, and I haven't since. It was a terrible experience. We were there until 9 p.m., I lost half my commission, and I failed my clients by not showing them the value I could bring. I made mistakes on this transaction, as all rookies will. But by removing myself from the communication process, I was not able to correct any misconceptions or problems as they came up. I've never made the mistake of letting buyers and sellers talk freely again.

For about half the deals you're involved in, real estate will come very easily. The buyer will pay cash and write an offer on the first property she sees. The inspection will come back with some minor issues that the seller immediately takes care of, there won't be any issues with the appraisal, and the property is closed without any headaches.

Then there will be the other half, for which nothing goes right. Others will make mistakes, you'll realize just how lazy people can be, someone will cross ethical boundaries, and you'll find yourself being yelled at for no fault of your own.

Remember this: if real estate were always easy, you wouldn't have a job. Real estate is complicated, and some transactions will turn nightmarish. And that's ultimately great news for you and your career. Learn to look forward to the problems in real estate and become an expert at solving them to help your clients and earn more commissions.

The 11 Worst Mistakes on a Contract

Few agents can actually write up a contract correctly. One of the best things you can do for your client is to learn the right way to write and respond to a contract. It signals professionalism and assures your client you really know what you're doing, resulting in a better price for your client. Here are the worst mistakes I see regularly on contracts:

1. Confusing the underwriter and the title company. The title company and the underwriter are not the same entity. When you fill out most contracts, there is a space to clarify who the title company is and who you prefer to issue title insurance (some title companies have more than one underwriter, so choose your client's preferred provider).

2. Leaving blanks on a contract. Be very careful about leaving blanks anywhere on a contract. They can be easily filled in and overlooked during negotiations and cause a problem down the road. Instead of leaving it blank, put "N/A" or "none" in the blank, as appropriate.

3. Representing more than one client. As one agent, unless you're a single broker firm, you cannot represent a seller and buyer by yourself. If there is an intermediary relationship, two different agents need to represent each prospect. If you're already representing the seller, and the buyer asks you to write a contract, you are still just representing the seller as your client (though you can help the buyer as a customer). Many experienced agents still get confused over the way this should be set up, but it's important to get it right on the contract. Make sure you understand the intermediary relationship and which side you fall on for a particular transaction, and mark it appropriately.

4. Separate written agreements for commission. On many contracts, there is a blank where you can state whether the sellers or buyers are paying a commission and to whom they will pay it, but it should be filled in only if there is not a separate written agreement. This is stated in bold letters right above the signature blanks, yet it's still one of the most problematic areas of a contract. I've had to argue about this clause in the contract with lawyers despite what it plainly states.

5. Commission. If you need to fill out the blanks because there is no separate listing agreement, make sure you don't also fill out the co-broker percentage blank too. If the other broker is paying you 3 percent of the commission, and you fill out the blanks at the bottom saying that seller will pay you 3 percent and the other broker 3 percent, then you are saying the listing broker will get no commission. The seller will pay you 3 percent, and then the listing broker will give you his commission of 3 percent. This is a common mistake, but it's easily fixed. Only one blank or the other should be filled out, never both, except in a very special circumstance. I have never needed to use both blanks—it's possible it could come up, though very unlikely.

6. Not providing the seller's disclosures before the contract is effective. There are strict timelines to adhere to on the contract, and the seller's disclosure language can really hurt your seller if you don't get it to the other party in a timely manner. Don't allow the contract to say, "Seller will provide disclosures in X days." In Texas, if the seller fails to provide in the correct amount of time, the buyer can opt out of the contract at any time before closing and have his earnest money protected.

7. Not providing the survey and double-checking what you put on the contract. Provide the survey upfront and be careful what you check on the contract. The misunderstanding about surveys and who pays for them still comes up often, even with experienced agents. If you commit to providing an existing survey as a seller's agent on a contract, you must provide one. After it's signed, you cannot tell the buyer that your seller doesn't have a survey and that the buyer needs to purchase one. You must provide a survey if you say you are going to, even if it means buying a brand-new one.

8. Not offering an exchange. In many places on a contract, you will be offering one thing in exchange for another. For example, on the option period, the buyer requests a period of days to look over the property more thoroughly. One common mistake is for agents not to offer anything in exchange for that time period.

Make sure you at least put a nominal amount of money for anything like that, even if it's only ten dollars. This mistake is also common on any non-realty items. For an agreement to be binding, each party should be exchanging something of value with the other.

9. Filling out the special provisions. As an agent, you have to be extremely cautious when adding anything to a standard contract. Always remember, and state, that you are an agent and not a lawyer. Don't tell your client that something is binding just because you have it in special provisions. Sadly, there are many, many examples of this, and you have probably run into some yourself. Here's just one: I had an agent who was buying just one part of the land from a seller. The seller wanted to restrict against chickens (I work in farm and ranch real estate, and this comes up all the time). The seller's agent put "no chickens" in special provisions, but nothing was added to the deed and nothing was formalized as restrictions. Now that the contract has closed, those restrictions don't exist anymore.

Another tip: when you communicate with your client anything that has legal implications, do it via text message or email so that you can save it and have a record. Verbal conversations are easy to forget over time, so having a written record is key to protecting yourself when something happens down the road. If your client asks for an explanation or a change that only a lawyer should make, respond in writing and recommend a lawyer.

10. Knowing what the default language says. Minerals often come up in my market. Sellers want to keep their minerals when they sell, but buyers want the minerals to come with the land. We spend more time negotiating minerals than any other point on the contract except for price. The default for a farm and ranch contract if minerals aren't mentioned is that the sellers will convey everything they own. If they want to reserve anything, then

they have to be proactive and add a mineral addendum to cover themselves on this. I've seen this mistake many times, and it's not only for minerals. Know what the defaults in the contract are so that you can both protect your client and use it to your client's advantage.

11. Countering too much. Only counter what's necessary. Don't get cute with seller contributions, buyers paying closing costs, or any other odd counters unless you absolutely have to. It won't fool anyone, and you're only hurting your client when you make a counter that way. If the other party has to spend three hours with his client explaining what your counter even means, you're falling down on your job. Both your offer and your counter should be as clean as possible. Unless it's absolutely necessary, try to counter only one point on a contract. Make it very easy for the other party to understand what they're getting into. If it takes only one initial, then you have a much better chance of getting it done than if you make it complicated.

Bonus Tip #15:

When I first started real estate, my grandmother made me fill out blank contracts over and over again. It wasn't a lot of fun, but when it came time to write a contract in front of a client, I was glad I had the experience. As a new agent, you should make it a priority to know your contracts backward and forward.

Here are just a few of the reasons why:

1. *It's not that hard. Real estate contracts are not rocket science. Just sit down and learn them.*
2. *Knowing your stuff really well is a great way to ease the tension and stress when someone is making a huge decision.*

3. When you make a stupid mistake on a contract, it's a dead giveaway to the agent on the other side you don't know what you are doing. It will be ten times worse once your client realizes it.

4. Writing up an offer live in front of someone is a must. You will sell more property, a lot more property, just by acquiring the skill of writing a contract.

5. Writing a contract is also a great closing technique, one of the three I use regularly.

6. It's your responsibility as an agent to be competent and able to protect your client in every way. Knowing how to write contracts correctly and quickly is a critical factor in this duty.

Knowing the standard contracts well should be the baseline for competence in a real estate transaction. If you're ever involved in a legal dispute, and you probably will be, contract law will likely determine the outcome of your case. Pay attention to the little things and learn your contracts well. It won't take long, and you'll be rewarded for your knowledge many times over.

The #1 Secret
to Real Estate Success

The hardest task in real estate is earning the right to be interviewed by sellers planning to list their property. Getting in front of sellers and convincing them to interview you is the key to success. When you earn that right through your personal connections or your marketing efforts, don't waste the opportunity.

When you're called in for an interview, what should you do to ensure you win the listing? Here are a few strategies I've used over the years that work well:

- Review the influence principles outlined earlier in this book. Think through how you can apply each principle to your interaction with the client.
- Make a great first impression. From the moment you walk in the door, the interview has started; everything you say or do matters.
- Prepare more than your competition. Have the square footage memorized, print the aerial photo, research the deed if you can, have a working knowledge of recent sales near the subject property, and have a listing agreement already filled out.
- Create an opportunity to go back to the property so that you get a chance to meet with the potential client twice. Know

the comparable properties in case you have to come up with a value on the fly, but ideally you want to view the house and get an idea of the condition. Then take a couple of days and come back with a full report. Most agents won't take the time to do this. However, meeting with the sellers twice shows professionalism and increases the likelihood they will hire you.

- Go first or last. Typically, you don't need to worry about being stuck in the middle between listings because sellers will rarely interview more than two agents for a listing. But, just in case, try to go either first or last. I prefer to be first because it gives me the chance to get a listing signed and have them cancel the other appointments. Also, if I'm first, I can make sure I still make the last impression by coming for my follow-up visit after their last interview.
- Define the questions. I have an interview worksheet I give to my listing prospects that has the ten most important questions they should ask an agent. Defining the conversation this way helps you to be prepared and gives them the tools to ask the right questions to others they interview.
- When you walk into the room, be aware of any material or notes from other agencies. Knowing who your competition is can be a large advantage. Once you know who they are, you can highlight the differences that make your business stand out from theirs.
- There are two approaches you can use when leaving information with a client. Some agents give a book's worth of printouts and paper; some have just a few documents. I prefer a few key documents so that they know what I want them to focus on. Keeping the handouts at a minimum also helps to highlight your company as straightforward and organized if the competition gives them four hundred pages of information they'll never read.

- Print out and bring recent testimonials with instructions on how to find more online. Use social proof as much as you can even during a private meeting.

- On all of my listing appointments, I bring a one-page document that highlights the reasons clients should choose me and my company. Think through the absolute best reasons anyone should hire you and work on creating a simple, one-page document you can give to anyone.

- Bring your client a gift at the second meeting as a thank-you for the interview. If you aren't able to get a second interview, send something in the mail immediately following your first interview. Engage the principle of reciprocity.

- Find ways to improve their listing. As you walk around the property, point out things that the sellers could do to increase the selling price. Show your value as an agent by immediately helping them make more money on their property. Many agents will gush over how much they like a listing without ever critiquing any part of it. Separate yourself by being genuine but also by helping them make good decisions about staging. Help them get the most value from their sale starting at your first meeting.

- Don't be afraid to bring in a partner. During an interview, if I realize one of our other agents would make a great partner on this property and help seal the deal, I will gladly bring him or her in to help. Giving up part of your listing commission to make sure you win the listing is a winning strategy. Know the other agents' strengths and weaknesses and start working on collaborating with those who can be helpful for your business.

- Accept anything that sellers offer you. Whether it's water, a snack, or anything else, accepting what is offered will help you establish rapport.

- Pay attention to what you are wearing. One of my favorite techniques for winning listings is to dress how I will show the listing and to bring the equipment I will need. If I'm going to list a large-acreage property, I wear my boots, jeans, and a nice pressed shirt. I often bring my four-wheel-drive truck and pull an all-terrain vehicle behind it. Pointing out your preparedness for showings and having the right equipment can be a big advantage, especially when your competition shows up in Italian loafers or high heels.

- As you prepare for your presentation, you should answer these three questions:
  - What do you want the seller to know?
  - What do you want them to feel?
  - What do you want them to do?
- Make your presentation personal. Agents often speak in platitudes that don't mean anything. If you get the opportunity to talk about your family, your history, or why you're really in this business, tell them the story. Show them pictures of your family and your kids. Make your company real, and it will be harder for them to choose someone else over you.

You will develop your own listing style over time and find ways to highlight your unique strengths. View each listing appointment as a challenge, one that will determine if you're moving in the right direction or not. I take each appointment personally, and if I don't win the listing, then I let the sting sink in. Use your natural competitive edge and don't allow any excuses when you lose a listing. Ruthlessly evaluate yourself and decide on what changes you will make next time.

Even now, I catch myself growing complacent after a few successful appointments. I won't print off the listing agreement, or I'll forget to bring the testimonials. Losing a listing I know I should have won is a reminder to go back to the basics and make sure I do everything in my power to win the listing.

Bonus Tip #16:

An easy way to stand out from the competition is to take great photographs. Unless you have a camera that costs most than $1,000 and you've taken photography classes, hire out your listing photos to a professional.

Getting the best photos on a property has a number of benefits, but most importantly it will help your clients get a premium on their home. Just taking great pictures can get more people in the door, create more interest, and encourage people to make offers faster because they know it looks great online.

When you choose pictures for your listing, highlight the best of the property. You don't need multiple pictures of every room; choose the best of what's out there. The goal with pictures is to whet someone's appetite to see the home in person, not to be a substitute for seeing the home.

Remember that buying a home is an emotional decision. When people walk into a house for the first time, they have a visceral, emotional reaction about whether they like it. The pictures that you present online should convince them to see the property, but they should also prime prospects to be on the lookout for features they like about it. Typically, buyers will make a decision about a property in the first thirty seconds of walking in. They spend the rest of their time in the house looking for reasons to back up what their gut is already telling them.

The Four Ways to Make Money on a Property

One of the best ways you can make yourself more valuable to a buyer is by proving your market knowledge and helping them make a smart purchasing decision. The goal of this chapter is to explain one of my favorite techniques for valuing properties on the fly and determining whether they're a good investment. I developed this from a few different real estate books I read when I first started selling, and it has remained one of the most valuable tools I use.

The following four principles are the only ways that you can make money on a property. If you can explain these principles to your client clearly and show whether the properties they're interested in are good investments, you will sell a lot more property.

Buy the Property under Market Value

If a house is worth $200,000 and you can pick it up for $150,000, you're already ahead of the game. These deals can be hard to find, but there are more out there than you think. Here are some tips for finding potentially undervalued deals:

- Look for weird real estate signs when you're driving around. One of the best investments I made resulted from a sign on a country road from a real estate company I had never heard of.

Turns out, the seller was listing the property as a favor to his family and was not advertising it in any way besides putting a sign out. It was a lot of work to purchase the property—it had thirty-six different owners despite being only thirty-four acres. After almost a year in escrow, we finally closed on it. Six months later, we sold it for an $80,000 profit before I even had a chance to list it.

- Watch the bad agents. There's not a nice way to say this: there are some really bad agents in every market who tend to underprice property. I love watching out for these agents and seeing what they list because there are often good deals. These agents haven't kept up with current market trends well enough, or have such a pessimistic view of a particular property that they underprice it.

- Measure it if it feels wrong. If a house feels larger than it's being advertised for, measure it. The second home we bought was actually 25 percent larger than it was advertised as (and on the tax rolls for). Fortunately, the agent had priced it based on the lower square footage. We essentially got 25 percent of that home for free. This is true for both land and homes.

- Look for bad aerials. I work in the land market quite a bit, and one of my favorite things to look at are long, skinny properties. These tend to look really bad online because they're so long and narrow, but many of them show well in person. Get boots on the ground when you see a property with a weird aerial. Many others pass before they even look at them, and there may be an opportunity for a great purchase.

- Look for terrible photos. If a property has really bad pictures, then it's one I want to see in person. Terrible pictures usually result in artificially low activity and may present an opportunity for a great deal. Most of the time, the pictures will accurately reflect the property, and the trip out there will be a waste of time. But one time out of ten, you'll find something worth making an offer on, either for yourself or your clients.

- Look for distressed owners and sales. When people think of buying property at under market value, they look for distressed properties first. In my experience, these sellers are pretty rare, and it's even more rare to hear about them before they've sold. There are investors in every city targeting these sellers through billboards, direct mail, seminars, and more. If you hear about one early, jump on it.

- Remember that as an agent, your job is to solve someone's most pressing problem. Sometimes price is secondary to unloading the property. The best deal I've come across like this was 120 acres next door to one of my listings. The neighbor had tried to sell to my client, but the sale didn't make sense for him at the time. So the neighbor approached me. I paid my client a nice referral fee, bought the property for about 50 percent of its market value, and packaged it together with the other listing.

- Buy an undivided interest in a property. This is a special case, but there are times when there are multiple owners of a property and they all disagree over whether it's time to sell. Often the holdouts drag their feet, and the other property owners get frustrated and just want to be done with it. In this case, you can buy an undivided interest in the property as an investment strategy.

  This strategy is great because you can typically buy the property at 40–60 percent of the value. The downside is that you will share an interest in the property with someone who may not be ready to sell or use the property in the same way as you. There is a process by which the courts can order an equitable partition of land if an agreement cannot be reached, and sometimes this is the only avenue left to make a deal work.

- Look at properties that have been on the market a long time. When I don't have any properties I'm targeting, I often look at properties online and sort by those that have been listed the longest. This is a great way to find overlooked deals. Most of the time, the sellers will be a lot more eager to sell and negotiate if their property has been on the market a long time.

- Think outside the box. If you typically focus on residential, look at commercial properties. You may be able to apply your unique expertise to a market segment you haven't been focusing on for one reason or another. One of my favorite investments, even though it has yet to earn me a dime, is a building I bought in the middle of downtown. It was a tiny retail store on a quiet street, and we bought it without knowing what we would do with it. It's become a gathering place for many different groups, including churches, book clubs, and investors. Though we have only used it ourselves, I consider it one of the best investments I've ever made.

Capital Improvements

Make capital improvements on the property when you can. Simply put, capital improvements are improvements that will bring you more value than they cost. There are many factors to consider when you calculate the value of an improvement on a property, but here are a few key ones:

- Landscaping. Consistently, no matter what area of the country you live in, landscaping has one of the highest returns. Beware that it is easy to overspend on landscaping, so don't overdo it. Primarily consider two things: What kind of lead picture do you want when you list the property one day, and what do you want the first impression to be when someone drives up to the house?
- Kitchens and bathrooms. Along with landscaping, these areas often yield your highest returns. Buyers tend to overestimate what it costs to get these rooms remodeled, and you can use that to your advantage. Simple things to consider:
  - Will it be easy to switch out countertops? Will butcher block look good? What about another inexpensive countertop?

- Can you paint the cabinets rather than replace them?
- Can you replace only cabinet doors if painting won't work?
- Can you upgrade the hardware for a new look?
- Can you update appliances, sinks, and fixtures to make a big difference?
- Can you install something obvious that is missing, such as a dishwasher?
- Can you put in new, inexpensive flooring, such as vinyl?
- Visit an IKEA kitchen showroom and see what ideas you get. They're often very inexpensive compared to other places, and you can get some great ideas. For example, look for a portable island you can add to the kitchen to increase counter space and break up the different areas.
- Can you switch out bathroom fixtures?
- Can you paint badly colored tile in the bathroom instead of replacing it?
- Can you change out window coverings?

• Pictures. When I talk to people who aren't familiar with real estate, they're often surprised that you can actually make money on a property just by changing the marketing. Small things can make a huge difference to the bottom line of any sale. Taking better pictures is an inexpensive capital improvement that can instantly increase value.

• Wood floors and shiplap walls. Wood floors and shiplap (horizontal wood planks) are very popular in my area. One of the easiest ways to improve a home is simply exposing what's already in place. I have simply pulled up carpet and lightly refinished the floors in multiple homes, and it's instantly increased value. The same is true of shiplap walls and even beadboard ceilings. Here are some easy ways to look for hidden value hiding underneath the current finishes:

- If you suspect wood floors are underneath the carpet, look in the closets and at the edges to see if there are any loose corners you can pull up easily. If the house has a pier-and-beam foundation, you may be able to get under the house and look up to see what the flooring is.

- ◉ Often when shiplap walls are covered, no one bothers to cover them up in the closest. You can also tap on the walls to hear if they are solid. Unfinished shiplap is great and can improve the home once painted, but it does take work. You'll often have to remove cheesecloth wallpaper first. If that's the case, you'll find a lot of tack nails and frayed strings in multiple places. I get rid of them by nailing the tack nails in until the wall is smooth, then using a blow torch to quickly burn off the strings. It requires caution, but it's a lot easier than trying to remove all the frayed areas.

- ◉ Once that's done, you will need at least two coats of primer and then one or two coats of paint depending on the color. Make sure your client is aware of the work it will take to do it right, but also find some finished examples to show them. It takes work but will really pay off.

- ◉ Beadboard ceilings are another positive. Again, closets are a great place to look up and see what is there. Also, check the inside of upper kitchen cabinets if they go all the way to the ceiling. Often you'll see the original ceiling there.

- Learn what each item will cost in your area. When you show a home to clients and explain how to easily improve the value of a home, you prove your expertise and teach them how to make a good investment. I highly recommend you start using local contractors for jobs and pricing them out, even if you want to do the work yourself.

  You will learn who to trust, who gives the best value for the price, and who to recommend as the right contractor to your clients. Knowing how to solve problems, redo items in the house, and estimate a cost is a huge competitive advantage.

- Look at the land. Sometimes there are ways to make capital improvements to increase the value outside the home as well. If the lot is oversized, investigate an easy way to split up the property. Often, if you can create an extra lot and sell it separately, you will triple the value of the lot you split off.
- Find a home that includes the lot next to it for free. This setup is a great way to find a good deal. Your client can add another home on the extra lot or sell it separately in the future.
- Likewise, if you're looking at raw land, look for opportunities to divide and sell it in multiple transactions. This will always increase the value and can be a great way to narrow down the options to the best investments.
- Look for properties on which the home has no value. Every once in a while, you'll see a listing that has no pictures of the home on the property or explicitly states that the home has no value. Homes are rarely too far gone to renovate. If you find a home that you can essentially pick up for free, you can fix it up and do really well. This is one of the highest value ways to locate a property with a lot of upside on capital improvements.
- Remove the junk. Often, buyers will overestimate what it costs to clean up a property. If a property has a lot of junk that just needs to be removed, explain to your client that just getting rid of the eyesores or the dilapidated buildings may increase the value of the whole property.

As you can see, there are many capital improvements that can make a huge difference to your bottom line. Consider all your options when you're helping a buyer make a decision on a property. Easy fixes can make the property a lot more attractive.

Make Income on the Property

The third way to make money is to monetize at least some portion of the property. The easiest and most common way to do this is to rent out either part or all of it, but there are also some other creative ways to use property for income.

- Rent out the property. The most common way to make money on a property is to rent out part or all of it. If your client is looking for a primary residence and is willing to rent out part of their property for additional income, look for properties that have a guest house, a garage apartment, or a mother-in-law suite. Buying a property and renting out a portion of it is a great way to cover most of your expenses while the value grows.
- Rent out the whole property. If your client is an investor, then he'll focus on renting from the beginning. Most investors will have their own unique set of criteria for valuing rentals, but you should have a standard formula you use as well. At a minimum, you should know the following about the rental market in your area to advise them.
  - What is the average rental price per month in your area?
  - How long does a rental typically stay vacant?
  - What's the top of the market for rentals in the area?
  - Are there any unique restrictions in the area that your buyer should be aware of? (For example, many areas are cracking down on homes rented to multiple people who aren't family members.)
  - Is there a better return in your area for monthly rentals or VRBO (Vacation Rental by Owner)? Why?
- Know the basics of what an investor is looking for. Briefly, most investors like a 1 percent per month return on purchase plus remodel price. So, if an investor pays $90,000 for the house and $10,000 to get it ready, it should rent for a mini-

mum of $1,000 a month. I highly recommend you listen to a few episodes of the *BiggerPockets* podcast to become more conversant with what investors are looking for.

- Mineral income. One of the more common ways to make money on property in our area is to obtain the minerals on a property. Though it's hard to find minerals these days, it's still possible to secure them on the right property. When your client purchases a property, you should insist on getting all or part of the minerals if at all possible. When you sell, you should insist on keeping them while being willing to waive your right to surface production. If surface rights (the rights of an oil and gas company to ingress and egress the property and build on the surface) are not conveyed with the property, expect the value to drop by 20–40 percent.
- Mineral rights are complicated, and laws will vary from state to state. Talk to a local oil and gas lawyer to figure how to best serve your clients. I have a few clients who buy land to get the minerals, and then they flip the rest of the land. If you can find clients like that, you will increase your sales fast if you know what to look for.
- Farm income. While it's typically minimal, it's always possible to lease out part of the property for cattle or hay. Current rates are low, typically in the tens of dollars per acre per year, but there are still a lot of advantages to doing this. As a landowner, you can avoid fence maintenance and fertilization cost while having someone keep an eye on the property for free. Plus, you can get an agricultural tax exemption where applicable.
- Exemptions. Learn what the going rates are in your area and what exemptions are available. Sometimes even a little bit of income or less time maintaining the property is enough to tip the scales and make the deal worth it for the right buyer.

There are a number of unusual ways to make money on a property that will rarely apply, but are still worth being aware of.

- Commercial water lease. On the right property, these can be very lucrative. Water is becoming more and more valuable. Be aware of the local water rights laws in your area. Many different oil companies are securing water leases because of the inordinate amount of water necessary for fracking, and many cities who are running low on water supply try to secure leases from land around them.
  - ⊚ Be aware. Advise your client that a long-term commercial water lease will devalue the property. Figure out what kind of income it will generate over time and see if it's worth it. It will often be lucrative in the right area, but a close comparison is always warranted. One of my clients was able to purchase a 400-acre ranch in Texas and then sell the water rights the day after closing for more than he paid for the whole property.
- Solar farms. These are becoming more and more popular every year. Many solar companies are looking for land that has very little elevation or slope change, is at least 70 acres, and has large power lines on the property that they can feed into. Typical solar leases can be $1,500 an acre per year for a 30-year lease. For the right piece of land, this can be a boon. Taking an unattractive, flat piece of land with a power line eyesore and seeing the potential is a skill that will help you sell more property if you can find the right place.
- Hunting leases. On the right property, you may be able to lease the land for hunting. Often you can lease it to multiple people depending on the size.
- Gravel income. This is a rare case, but it does come up. Gravel and dirt companies' biggest expenses are gas from hauling

material, so if there is a property suitable for gravel production that is close to an area about to grow, it can provide a significant source of income. This is a specialized type of production, and you should connect with a gravel buyer who really knows what they are looking for. Typically land near a river has a higher chance of being suitable, but even that is not a sure thing.

  ⊚ Developing gravel from a property will certainly lower the value, but it can be one of the most lucrative types of production for the property owner as well. On the right property, royalty checks can be six figures a month for more than 20 years.

- Build additional rental facilities. When looking at property with a client, be aware of any opportunities to easily add rental facilities as well. You might be able to convert an outbuilding into an additional rental facility. Turning the barn into a wedding venue is one example that has worked for clients in the past.

- Trading places. In some cases, when your buyers are trying to decide between one house or another, you can point out that one of them is more suitable for short-term leases. That knowledge often tips the scales. In our area, vintage homes are desirable for short leases. There are many different websites that help you trade places with someone from a different part of the country or the world, and having a unique property near city services will be more attractive, if this is something your client would consider.

Rental income is often the least likely of the four principles that buyers think about, but educating yourself on some of these different ideas should add to your bottom line. Show your buyers that you don't have to be a landlord to make income on a property. Thinking outside the box and figuring out ways to earn income on a property can be the difference between a sale and a missed opportunity.

Market Appreciation

Market appreciation is the fourth principle of making money in real estate. Real estate markets can be difficult to predict, but there are rules of thumb that you need to be aware of and communicate to your clients when they're looking at a property.

- Buy in a growing area. One of the best ways to make sure a home appreciates is to pay attention to the laws of supply and demand. Real estate booms don't often happen overnight; you can see where the trends are heading long before they actually reach you. Keep track of growth projections and relative growth history for other areas close by. Knowing how fast one town grew in the last census compared to three other similar cities is valuable information for your clients.
- Buy something they aren't making more of. There are often homes with unique features that will become scarce over time. These could include homes within walking distance of a downtown area, homes on large lots, antique homes, and even properties with great views. If you find a property that includes one or more unique features, then the property is better positioned for market appreciation.
- Be aware of developments nearby. Often when larger developments come to an area, many people know what's coming long before it's actually built. Developments will often boost an area's market value, but not always. If you own a home near a downtown area that is about to be revitalized, then it's a good bet your value will increase. If you own a 30-acre farm next to an area about to be developed into an RV park, your value may decrease.
- Give it time. When someone is trying to make the decision between renting and buying, I always tell clients that if they aren't sure they'll be in an area at least two years, it's better

to rent. If they know they'll be in the area for longer than two years, it's better to buy. Owning a property for that short of a time doesn't give market appreciation enough time to work its magic.

- Be wary of new. Many of your clients will want to buy a brand-new home. If anyone buys a new home in a neighborhood and then has to move sooner than expected, they may be in trouble. If the same neighborhood just opened another section of brand-new homes, now they have to compete against them. Financing terms are often more generous for brand-new homes as well, so they'll have to factor that into listing price. Betting on market appreciation for a new home is a risk that should be carefully weighed by anyone who may be forced to move earlier than they would like to.

Market appreciation is often the least predictable of the four ways to make money in real estate, but there are some factors that will point you in the right direction. When I'm personally looking for a home or investment property, I like to hit at least three of these four principles. If you can effectively explain to your clients how to make money on real estate by understanding these principles, you will help them recognize a good deal when they see one.

Helping someone buy a property that is obviously a great deal is rewarding, and your clients will be grateful. A deal only becomes great when the client decides to sell it one day; therefore, helping your buyers find awesome deals now is laying the groundwork for great listings in the future.

Now . . . Go Sell Some Property

My goal for this book is to share some of the best practices that have worked for me. Reading a book like this can feel like drinking from a fire hose because there are a lot of ideas and actions to take, but if you use even a few tips within these pages, you will increase your bottom line. When I started selling properties, I read many books on real estate but never found one I really liked. Many offer advice on practices I would never try, like cold calling and going after for-sale-by-owners, but none offered actionable steps to grow a business for long-term success.

My learning curve was long, full of trial and error and many missteps. By sharing some of my mistakes and failures, I hope to help you avoid similar pitfalls and move toward success much faster. New agents often want training and the assurance of someone looking over their shoulder. I tell all our new agents that they need to take responsibility for their own education and training but come to me if there are any gaps I can help fill. No one is going to care about your business like you do, and if you wait for your company or your broker to teach you the right things instead of taking the initiative, you will fall behind.

This book is a step in the right direction. You should now have the tools you need to set goals, follow through on them, focus on your energy, craft presentations based on sound psychology, and even negotiate with the best agents out there. If you're just starting out, you now have a head start on the real lessons in real estate. Take the long view and commit to building your business the right way.

My perspective changed when I bought the business from my grandparents, and now my focus is shifting more toward helping other agents succeed rather than growing my own client list. I would love to hear from you and know what you liked about this book. Please contact me at Brad@BeversRealEstate.com.

Recommended Reading

Below are books I recommend all agents read. I used many of them to research this book. If you want more book recommendations, I write a newsletter once a month that has reviews of all the books I've read the previous month. They're not all real estate books (I read a wide range of genres), but you will find something to like each month. Send me an email at Brad@BeversRealEstate.com.

Never Split the Difference by Chris Voss. I rarely reread books. I tend to take really good notes and write my own summaries when I'm finished so that I have what I need from then on. This book is an exception; I just finished reading it for the fourth time in four years. Buy this in print and audiobook format and study it. It's by far the best book on negotiating that I've read.

Captivate by Vanessa Van Edwards. If you want to learn how to keep conversations going easily, how to assess other personalities instantly, and how to approach new people at a party, get this book. Van Edwards also has some excellent classes on CreativeLive that I highly recommend.

The Obstacle Is the Way by Ryan Holiday. A great book to read, especially when you are first starting out. Real estate is a hard business and you will run into many roadblocks, but if you can keep going, you will be rewarded. This book was very helpful for me during a tough time in real estate.

The Power of Full Engagement by Jim Loehr and Tony Schwartz. The message of this book is simple: energy is a lot more important than time for entrepreneurs. It's worth reading for practical tips on increasing your energy levels in different areas.

Miracle Morning Millionaires by Hal Elrod and David Osborne. If the measure of a self-help book is how much it actually changes you, then this is the best one I've read. It offers a great framework for a morning routine that can change your life if you follow it. The head start this routine gives me is extremely valuable. I can't recommend this one highly enough. Note: Do *not* buy the *Miracle Morning for Real Estate Agents*. It's a terrible book.

The 4-Hour Workweek by Timothy Ferriss. This book has influenced my business over the years more than any other. It helped me brainstorm ways to make ends meet when times were tough, think through working smarter rather than harder, and set big goals. Buy this book and try it. You will like it.

The Personal MBA by Josh Kaufman. If you want to fill the holes in your business knowledge, start here. This book saved me from going back to school to get an MBA and is an invaluable resource I go back to again and again.

The Power of Moments by Chip Heath and Dan Heath. The Heath brothers have written some great books. In fact, I wholeheartedly recommend all of them. Start with this one. It will help you think through unique ways to present your business. It's extremely helpful and has the power to change your business.

The Ultimate Sales Letter by Dan S. Kennedy. I'm pretty sure I own every book Dan Kennedy has written at this point. His approach to marketing is the opposite of brand building, and his techniques have been extremely helpful in my business. This is a great place to start because you'll learn his philosophy and also gain a very practical tool you can use right away. If you want to be a good agent, you have to get better at marketing.

The 33 Ruthless Rules of Local Advertising by Michael Corbett. I've returned to this book more times than I can remember. It offers a very helpful and unique take on marketing. There's no junk in this book, no wasted time with brand-building advertising. My biggest takeaway I still apply today is that if you don't already know why someone contacted you, you're too late. Asking them why they came in or called is a waste of time and won't tell you much.

The 22 Immutable Laws of Marketing by Al Ries and Jack Trout. This is a short book that will help you think through one of the most important aspects of your own marketing: positioning. Concise and to the point, the lessons in this book will stay with you long after you've read it.

The 48 Laws of Power by Robert Greene. If you want to prepare yourself to deal with agents who fight dirty, read this book. It exposes the secrets of power that many use to rise to the top. It will make you think differently about why some are successful and some aren't, and it should make you reexamine your own moral code and nail down exactly what you believe and how you will run your business.

The *BiggerPockets* Podcast. This is the first recommendation I make when people tell me they want to invest or learn more about investing. It's an excellent resource. Start anywhere and listen to what looks interesting. You will quickly get a masters-level education in real estate investing. There are some decent books that can complement it, some that the creators of the podcast have written, but the podcast is still by far the best resource.

How to Fail at Almost Everything and Still Win Big by Scott Adams. We have a limited time in our lives to read, and it took a lot of recommendations for me to finally pick up a book by the creator of *Dilbert* and read it. I'm glad I finally did. His story and philosophy of learning are very helpful. From diet to systems thinking to goal setting, this book will help you influence yourself to get more done.

Win Bigly by Scott Adams. Adams was one of the few people who predicted a Donald Trump presidential victory before the election. Thanks to him, I made $500 and won two steak dinners betting with friends. This book exposes the persuasion techniques that Trump used to win the election and will help show you the importance of psychology in sales thinking. Whether you agree with his politics or not, this book is a valuable read.

Influence by Robert Cialdini. If you're interested in learning more about human nature, how to influence others, or how to protect yourself from being influenced, get this book. Once you read it, you'll realize how many other books use this as a starting point, even decades after it was published.

Pre-Suasion by Robert Cialdini. A recent follow-up to his book on influence, this one is definitely worth picking up as well. It includes great anecdotes and advice on preparing to influence others. One of my favorite stories is about a security salesman who was outselling everyone else in the company. Cialdini shadowed him, trying to unlock the secret, but was baffled because he did very little different from the other salespeople. Then it dawned on him: the salesman would always forget a document in his car, excuse himself from the meeting to grab it, and let himself back into the house. This simple act transformed him from a salesman to a trusted friend who could let himself in.

To Sell Is Human by Daniel H. Pink. The premise of this book is that the death of sales has been greatly exaggerated. In fact, more than any other time, we are all in desperate need of sales skills. Pink offers a fresh take on sales with some great, actionable advice. Each chapter ends with practical steps you can take to implement the lessons learned.

The Introvert's Edge by Matthew Pollard. This is a sales book everyone should read. I wish it were titled differently because I think most people who don't consider themselves introverts will avoid it, but there is valuable information here for everyone. It offers great advice on building your own sales stories to help your businesses, along with other practical tools.

Following Through by Steve Levinson and Pete Greider. One of the best books I've read on forming habits and using human psychology on yourself to get things done. If you have trouble following through on your goals or if you wonder how to implement them faster and more effectively, get this short book.

80/20 Sales and Marketing by Perry Marshall. This book is like drinking from a fire hose. You will find tips on changing your mindset, ranking customers, focusing on what truly matters, and marketing effectively. It's a unique book; I haven't read anything else like it. With great tools and advice, it has the potential to help you grow your business quickly.

No B.S. Wealth Attraction in the New Economy by Dan S. Kennedy. Despite the clunky title, this one is really good. Each short chapter seeks to dismantle myths about money and show you a different way to think about it. Thinking about how money works is important in real estate for many reasons, but two stand out. First, as agents we need an abundance mindset: there is more than enough business out there for everyone; it's not a zero-sum game. Second, wealth (and sales) flow to those who don't seem to need it. The second your clients sense you need a sale to happen, you're in trouble.

Defeat Mega-Agents by Ryan Fletcher. I wanted to include at least one book on this list directed toward agents, and this is the one that stands out. Despite being written by someone who sold real estate for less than two years, Fletcher gives some great advice on growing your business in unique ways. If you want to try a direct-marketing model but have trouble getting started, get this book and take his lessons to heart. You will come away with some great ideas on how to stand out in your market.

Rich Dad, Poor Dad by Robert T. Kiyosaki. When you talk to real estate investors, this book comes up again and again as the book that got them started. Personally, I didn't find it that compelling, but I have also seen how helpful it can be for many. If you want to take the plunge, this book will help you develop the mindset of an investor.

A Man in Full by Tom Wolfe. I wouldn't feel right if I didn't include at least one fiction book on this list. This book follows the transformation of a real estate mogul who discovers the ancient philosophy of Stoicism and embarks on a journey that will transform his life. Important lessons here for agents and anyone else who falls into the more-stuff trap.

Notes

Energy vs. Time

1. Richard Branson, quoted in Leah Ginsburg, "Mark Zuckerberg, Richard Branson and Mark Cuban All Agree That This One Habit Is Key to Success," CNBC.com Make It, May 28, 2017, https://www.cnbc.com/2017/05/28/mark-zuckerberg-and-richard-branson-exercise-is-key-to-success.html.
2. Dietrich Bonhoeffer, *Letters and Papers from Prison*, ed. Eberhard Bethge (N.p.: SCM Press, 1981), 7, Google Books.
3. Seneca, *On the Shortness of Life: Life Is Long If You Know How to Use It*, trans. C.D.N. Costa (New York: Penguin Books, 1997), Google Books.
4. Hal Elrod and David Osborn, *Miracle Morning Millionaires: What the Wealthy Do before 8AM That Will Make You Rich* (N.p.: Hal Elrod International, 2018), 43.
5. Andrew Perrin, "Slightly Fewer Americans Are Reading Print Books, New Survey Finds," Pew Research Center, October 19, 2015, http://www.pewresearch.org/fact-tank/2015/10/19/slightly-fewer-americans-are-reading-print-books-new-survey-finds/.

Everyone Is Selling Something

1. Plato, https://www.lifehack.org/articles/communication/wise-men-speak-because-they-have-something-say-plato.html, accessed May 24, 2019.

First Impressions

1. Vanessa Van Edwards, *Captivate: The Science of Succeeding with People*, (New York, Portfolio, 2017), 59.

Taking Action

1. Steve Levinson and Pete Greider, *Following Through*: A Revolutionary New Model for Finishing Whatever You Start, (Bloomington, Unlimited, 2007).
2. Timothy Ferriss, *The 4-Hour Chef: The Simple Path to Cooking Like a Pro, Learning Anything, and Living the Good Life* (Boston: New Harvest, 2012), 69.

Real Estate and Influence

1. Robert Cialdini, *Influence: The Psychology of Persuasion* (New York: Harper Collins, 2007), 3.
2. Michael V. Pantalon, *Instant Influence: How to Get Anyone to Do Anything—FAST* (New York: Little, 2011), 68.

The Psychology of Negotiation

1. Chris Voss, *Never Split the Difference* (New York: HarperCollins, 2016), 206.

How to Always Get a Full Commission

1. Timothy Ferriss, *The 4-Hour Workweek: Escape 9-5, Live Anywhere, and Join the New Rich* (New York: Crown, 2009), 55.

Searching for the Best Clients

1. Perry Marshall, *80/20 Sales and Marketing: The Definitive Guide to Working Less and Making More* (N.p.: Entrepreneur Press, 2013), 179–182.

About the Author

My name is Bradley Bevers and I'm a real estate broker in Chappell Hill, a small Texas town located midway between Houston and Austin. I've sold real estate full-time since I graduated from Texas A&M in 2004.

Despite starting off in the family business, I struggled in real estate for many years. It was hard to know exactly what to do and how to do it, and I did not get off to a fast start. I was able to sell almost three million dollars of real estate my first year, but then the market stalled, and I failed to sell even one million dollars for the next three years. Despite having a business degree and being a born entrepreneur, I made a lot of mistakes along the way and learned mostly through trial and error.

In 2017, I sold over seventeen million dollars of real estate. My income has gone up more than 20 times since those early years. Out of almost thirty agents, I've been the top producer in my company for six years in a row. Now, I want to share what I've learned so you can get a jump start on your own career.

If you're looking for a book that will give you the secret sauce to cold calling, social media prowess, or working for-sale-by-owner and expired listings, this book isn't for you. I've never made a cold call in my life, and I post on Facebook once or twice a year. If you want to make more money, build your reputation the right way, and avoid some of the pitfalls of selling real estate, then this is the book you're looking for.